Child Observation for Learning and Research

Theodora Papatheodorou and
Paulette Luff with Janet Gill

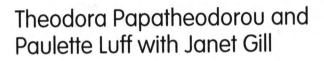

Routledge
Taylor & Francis Group

LONDON AND NEW YORK

First published 2011 by Pearson Education Limited

Published 2013 by Routledge
2 Park Square, Milton Park, Abingdon, Oxon OX14 4RN
711 Third Avenue, New York, NY 10017, USA

Routledge is an imprint of the Taylor & Francis Group, an informa business

ISBN: 978-1-4058-2467-5 (pbk)

British Library Cataloguing-in-Publication Data
A catalogue record for this book is available from the British Library

Library of Congress Cataloging-in-Publication Data

Papatheodorou, Theodora, 1953-
   Child observation for learning and research / Theodora Papatheodorou and Paulette Luff;
with Janet Gill.
      p. cm.
   Includes bibliographical references and index.
    ISBN 978-1-4058-2467-5 (pbk.)
1. Child development–Evaluation. 2. Early childhood education. 3. Ability–Testing. 4. Education.
I. Luff, Paulette. II. Gill, Janet. III. Title.

   LB1131.P266 2011
   372.21–dc22

2011015018

Typeset in 10.25/14pt Interstate Light by 73

Child Observation for Learning and Research

This book is dedicated to all our students, past and present, whose learning journeys inspired us to write this book

Contents

List of figures

List of tables

List of theorist boxes

List of theory and literature boxes

List of appendices

Preface

Background information

This book is based on our experiences as teachers in further and higher education teaching child observation. We have taught observation individually and together at different times for many years. We have different backgrounds and experience in childcare, education, social work and research bringing different perspectives to our teaching. Our diverse backgrounds meant that we had to go through a process of learning ourselves which required an examination of our professional and discipline-related knowledge and assumptions, and we negotiated them to arrive at shared understandings for teaching child observation as an active learning process.

We taught observation by asking students to conduct and record narrative observations with the aim of understanding children and their experiences. We provided guidelines for planning and conducting observations and supported students in making their own arrangements. We continued supporting them with weekly seminars, where students reflected on and discussed their observations. It was during these discussions that our learning continued as we appreciated the range of challenges experienced by the students, and we encountered their excitement and enthusiasm about what and how they had learned.

Some of the challenges experienced by students were of a practical nature at the stages of planning and the actual doing of observations (e.g. who to observe, where and when; how to gain access; how to respond to interruptions and unexpected incidents during observation). Others were of an ethical nature arising before and during observations (e.g. receiving informed consent; issues of anonymity and confidentiality; concerns about children and/or practice). Choosing observation methods, producing sound observational records (e.g. free from bias and judgemental language) and their analysis and interpretation presented further challenges. Often observations and subsequent reflections brought up strong emotions and feelings. Writing on observations and providing coherent arguments for conclusions also had its own challenges.

Mostly, observations themselves proved to be absorbing experiences, generating excitement and enthusiasm. Discussions and reflections in seminars became lively and exhilarating, leading to debates, alternative ideas and theoretical perspectives. These discussions enabled students to:

- make sense of their observations;
- recognise and understand theories, to see them from different perspectives and question them, in relation to their observations;
- examine and challenge their assumptions and preconceived ideas, receive peer feedback and deal with ambiguity and uncertainty;
- adopt a rigorous and systematic process in the course of their learning.

During these discussions we, the tutors, became aware that students were learning to become more self-reflective, self-aware, and sensitive to others. They dealt more confidently with the discussions and they seemed to be learning to relate theoretical ideas to their own observations. By reflecting on their own assumptions and knowledge, and addressing uncertainties and ambiguities, the students actively engaged with their own learning and started to make sense of themselves as learners.

It was our learning from these discussions that led us to incorporate explicitly this dimension of observation in our teaching of child observation. We recognised that not only observational skills are to be learned, and child study and settings to be understood, but also the process of self-learning needs to be explored and internalised. We developed a systematic and rigorous framework that focused on acquiring observational skills; making sense of the observed child or practice and recognising and questioning theory; and making sense of own learning.

The purpose of the book

This is a book about observation with a difference. While we have explained some of the methods and skills, strengths and pitfalls of the observation process, we have placed particular emphasis on observation as a tool for (i) experiential learning (Dewey 1997a; Kolb 1984), (ii) basis for reflection (Brookfield 1995; Dewey 1991; Gibbs 1988) and (iii) systematic analysis following research-oriented approaches (Delamont 2002) to reach conclusions that are well substantiated and argued, have personal meaning as well as currency among peers and professionals in the field.

The book is aimed as an aide for undergraduates and, especially, for those who enter higher education at different stages in their lives and professional careers, and bring with them diverse experiences. Committed to offering students a learning experience that is personally meaningful and has currency among peers and professionals in the field, our main aim is to offer a textbook which will facilitate undergraduates to make the best use of the opportunities offered through observation, and to join or rejoin academic study with confidence in order to acquire sound observational skills and use them to:

- advance their own understanding of children, their experiences and contexts;
- recognise and, if appropriate, question theory;
- understand how knowledge is constructed and become aware of their own role in this process;
- inform professional practice.

Structure and content of the book

The book is divided into two parts. The first part focuses on pre-observational issues, involving thinking about and careful planning and preparation for observations. It starts with an introductory chapter that explores the informal and formal use of observation for learning. The second chapter takes a historical overview of the development and use of observation as a tool for studying children, their context and educational practice. Chapter 3 outlines some of the most frequently used methods of observation, while Chapter 4 concentrates on practical issues of planning and making arrangements for observations. Ethical issues involved in the observational process are discussed in Chapter 5. The role of attitudes and the observer stance are dealt with in Chapters 6 and 7, respectively.

The second part of the book focuses on doing, reflecting, analysing and making sense of observations. More specifically, Chapter 8 discusses the actual conducting and recording of observations, while Chapter 9 explores reflection and the reflective process in observation. Chapter 10 details the process of systematic analysis of observational records. Analysis is further explored in Chapter 11, which also considers the process of interpreting observations. Chapter 12 focuses on the uses of observation as a research tool, while Chapter 13 considers writing on observations. The use of observation in childcare is addressed in Chapter 14. The book concludes with Chapter 15, which provides an overview of the observational process, its challenges and demands on self-awareness to become a powerful tool for learning.

Chapter features

Each chapter is designed to facilitate learning and starts with a brief summary of aims which outlines the key points to be discussed, followed by vignettes that draw attention to some of the issues that are explored. In some chapters we have included 'theorist' and 'theory' boxes, chosen for their relevance to learning and/or observational process. Figures to illustrate key concepts at a glance, and tables to summarise key points are also included, when appropriate. Each chapter ends with a concluding activity that offers readers the opportunity to reflect further and/or think about their own observation. Consistent with our commitment to experiential learning, some chapters are of a more practical nature, while others endeavour to introduce discipline-related concepts and ideas.

Clarifications and disclaimer

This book is intended as an academic text and, as such, contains a wide range of references to other literature. In some parts of the book, particularly those of a practical nature, we have kept specific references to a minimum to maintain the flow of the text. Where ideas are specific to particular authors, we have attributed these. We have, however, drawn much from our own experience of work with students and from knowledge we regard as being in the public domain.

We have used her/his in most places when referring to observers. This is to reflect the predominance of females in the discipline of early childhood studies and the early childhood profession while avoiding stereotyping or excluding male readers. For consistency in our writing, we have chosen to keep the same form when referring to children.

The vignettes come from observational studies, practice and research from our own research and/or by courtesy of students with whom we have worked. They have been anonymised and, when appropriate, modified to avoid deductive identification of observed individuals and settings. All names given are pseudonyms and any similarity with real situations is purely coincidental.

Acknowledgements

There are many people to whom we are indebted for the writing and completion of this book. First of all, the students we have taught, during the last two decades, and who have taught us most of what we know about observation. Their insightful comments, questioning attitude, enthusiasm and excitement have inspired us to write this book. Second, the students who allowed us to cite anonymously excerpts of their observations and writings in this book, and third all anonymous referees who made time to read initial and final drafts of this book and provide useful constructive feedback. You all know who you are; thank you all.

Our special thanks go to Nigel Lewin, who shared with us his childhood observations and learning, and allowed us to use one of them to discuss the informal use of observation, in Chapter 1 (Vignette 1.1). Our thanks go to 'Play to Z' for permission to use an observation excerpt from the *Sensory Play* project for analysis in Chapter 10. Our sincere thanks go to Catherine Yates, the commissioning editor, who has waited patiently for this long overdue completed manuscript.

Last but not least, Paulette and Theodora would like to acknowledge the generous sabbatical leave that both received from their employing institution, Anglia Ruskin University, during the academic year 2009-10. This leave made possible the completion of the manuscript.

Theodora Papatheodorou, Paulette Luff, Janet Gill

2011

Publisher's Acknowledgements

Picture Credits
The publisher would like to thank the following for their kind permission to reproduce their photographs:

(Key: b-bottom; c-centre; l-left; r-right; t-top)

Cornell University News Service: 58c; **Getty Images:** AFP 9c, FPG 19c, Popperfoto 24c; **Science Photo Library Ltd:** New York Public Library 6c, Ria Novosti/Science Photo Library 10c

Cover image: *Front:* **Getty Images**

Every effort has been made to trace the copyright holders and we apologise in advance for any unintentional omissions. We would be pleased to insert the appropriate acknowledgement in any subsequent edition of this publication.

Part I
Thinking about and planning for child observation

Chapter 1
Observation and learning

In this chapter we explore the role of observation in the learning process, both informal and formal, and discuss social constructivism as our theoretical framework for learning and knowledge construction. For this, we briefly explore what constitutes learning and some debates about how we learn, and consider various theories of learning before discussing social cultural constructivism as our model of understanding observation as a learning tool.

Vignette 1.1

In the garden, in early July, Nigel - the gardener - and I are having lunch. A wasp came and took a small piece of ham. It flew away and came back repeatedly for more helpings.

- Just watch it, said Nigel. It cuts small, perfectly rounded, pieces of ham the size of its head . . . This time of the year wasps go for meat.

- How do you know this? I asked surprised.

- Well, when I was a child, I used to observe them coming to our butcher's window, this time of the year . . . By August wasps go for the ripe, sweet fruits. I used to think as a child that the wasps ate meat because there were not any ripe fruits for them to eat. I now know that they take the meat to feed the grubs that produce sweet excretions which then are eaten by the wasps.

Vignette 1.2

My son, four years old, is sitting at the dining table with a piece of paper in front of him and his crayons. After some time and with much attention to detail, he drew a fish. He picked up his drawing and looked at it. He seemed satisfied with his work. He then put it down on the table. He looked at his crayons and chose a dark blue colour. He started scribbling on top of his picture, until the drawing of the fish was not visible. He is not happy with his picture, I thought. He always does this when he is not satisfied with his work. Such a perfectionist! But then I asked:

- So, what have you drawn there?

- Oh, it's a fish, but it's in the sea. So, you cannot see it now!

Introduction

Observation is what we constantly do in our everyday life; we observe physical and social phenomena as well as other people and, on the basis of these observations, we attempt to understand and make sense of the surrounding world.

We identify patterns, make associations between them, and form certain ideas of the things happening around us (as in Vignette 1.1) or we attribute thoughts and intentions and characteristics to observed individuals (as in Vignette 1.2). Although casual and informal, hastily conducted, and often merging evidence and opinion, our everyday observations gradually form our *folk* theories. These theories provide us with a system of connected assumptions and beliefs which form our source of knowledge about the world that we use to organise and make sense of new experiences (Bruner 1990).

Everyday observations, however, may also lead to habitual thinking, false assumptions and presumptions, and stereotypical thinking, if we fail to make meaningful connections (Dewey 1991). For example, was Nigel correct with his childhood claim that wasps went for meat? What was the underlying assumption of his claim? Was his assumption adequately substantiated? Similarly, have the mother's prior observations led her to habitual and stereotypical thinking about her son (he – her son – always does this; he is such a perfectionist)?

Dewey (1991) claimed that habitual observations may lead to 'lazy' thinking which makes it difficult for people to cope with incongruent information and difference. He argued that to make meaningful connections we need reflective and analytic modes of thinking that set us free from past routine and customary interpretations of our experience. He maintained that people need to reach a certain level of abstraction, that is, to move away from concrete experience and habitual responses, in order to think differently, learn new things and be liberated to follow alternative or new ideas.

Theorist box 1.1

John Dewey

John Dewey (1859–1952) was a prominent American philosopher and educational theorist whose work shaped much of the educational thinking in the twentieth century. He paid particular attention to the role of experience and reflection in human learning. He opposed the prevalent (at his time) knowledge transmission model of learning and, as a response, he proposed experiential learning as a framework that explained the development of knowledge as an adaptive human response to environmental conditions. Some of his influential books in education include: *How We Think* (1991); *Experience and Education* (1997a); *Democracy and Education* (1997b).

The significance of Dewey's comments cannot be underestimated, especially when we use observation as a purposeful and intentional learning tool. Indeed, for a long time observation has been used as a tool to offer concrete experiences to learn about something (e.g. child development; teaching and learning). Through the systematic, methodical and rigorous examination of the observations conducted we also begin to understand the learning process, that is, how to learn. To understand the learning process through observation, we will define the term learning in this chapter and briefly discuss the debates about how we learn. We will then explore the role of observation in learning through various theories of learning. We will conclude by discussing observation within socio-cultural constructivism and its role in the learning of students pursuing childhood studies.

What is learning?

It is difficult to define learning and, indeed, most researchers and theorists refer to the function and impact of learning rather than defining it. For example, Woolfolk et al. (2008:24) understand learning as the process that causes 'permanent change in knowledge and behaviour' through experience, while Lave and Wenger (1991:53) state that learning helps individuals to 'become [sic] a different person' through the possibilities offered within her/his social system or community. In general, these ideas about learning highlight the transformational nature of learning and emphasise the role of experience located within the learner's physical and social environment.

There are continuing debates about how learning is understood in formal education. Hargreaves (2004:27) states that, in education, learning is often described as the *acquisition of knowledge, skill and understanding,* and he also recognises that *learning how to learn* is equally important. The first view of learning implies that there is a body of knowledge and theories (e.g. child development, sociological theories etc.) considered to have general currency about our understanding of the world and, thus, they deserve to be transmitted from generation to generation. The latter view sees learning as a process where we use past and current knowledge and our own experience to change our ways of thinking and our behaviour. The first view of learning reflects the *knowledge transmission* model, while the latter the *knowledge construction* model of learning (Hargreaves 2004; McCormick and Paechter 1999; Dewey 1991).

In general, the knowledge transmission model assumes that learners change in thought and behaviour through their familiarisation and acquaintance with existing theories and literature; knowledge comes from outside. This view is reflected in early radical behaviourism and is better illustrated in Watson's (1930:104) claim, below:

> Give me a dozen healthy infants, well-formed, and my own specified world to bring them up in and I'll guarantee to take any one at random and train him to become any type of specialist I might select – doctor, lawyer, artist, merchant-chief and, yes, even beggar-man and thief, regardless of his talents, penchants, tendencies, abilities, vocations, and race of his ancestors.

Learning through observation

The determinism of external factors and the assumed passivity of learners however were soon challenged from within behaviourism (Bandura 1977; 1986; Skinner 1953; 1976). Bandura, in particular, with his social learning theory, maintained that as children grow their development is increasingly based on observation and imitation. He argued that children learn to regulate their own behaviours and actions by watching others around them and imitating their actions (Bandura 1977). He emphasised the role of children's cognitive capacity in discriminating the consequences of observed events and behaviours (Bandura 1986). His argument was that learning is not happening in a vacuum; instead, it takes place within a social context with learners exercising their cognitive abilities.

The role of cognition in children's learning has been central to early theories of constructivism. Piaget, for example, explained learning in terms of the child's capacity to construct knowledge through a gradual and evolving cognitive process throughout childhood. He saw children as emergent scientists, who, given the appropriate experiences, were capable to discover the principles that govern phenomena (Kail 2004; Vasta et al. 1999). Piaget's (2002) interest and focus was on understanding children's cognitive and mental processes in constructing their ideas, as they experimented with the resources available. His ideas attracted the interest of educationalists who introduced the notion of learning by doing through the availability of appropriate resources and gradually shifted attention from *learning that* (knowledge transmission) to *learning how* (knowledge construction) (Hargreaves 2004).

> ## Theorist box 1.2
>
> ### Jean Piaget
>
>
>
> Jean Piaget (1896–1980) is one of the most well-known and quoted developmental psychologists, whose work and ideas much influenced the field of education during the twentieth century. Piaget's initial studies were in biology and philoso-phy, which influenced his work in terms of the methodologies (observation) and the underlying concepts (e.g. adaptation, accommodation and assimilation) of his child development theory. Although his ideas were challenged and contested by some researchers, his work is considered as having founded the concept of constructivism and informed the learning and teaching approaches of many educational systems. Some of his most influential books include: *Play, Dreams and Imitation in Childhood* (1951); *The Origin of Intelligence in the Child* (1953); and *The Language and Thought of the Child* (2002).

Observation was a key tool for Piaget (2002) in understanding children's language and the cognitive processes involved in children's learning. He systematically observed his own children and conducted observational studies that were complemented with interviewing to understand how children think and arrive at their conclusions. Evidently, for Piaget observation was an essential tool to access children's thinking, but insufficient. As was also illustrated in Vignette 1.2 above, the observation alone led the mother to a misattribution; it was the child's explanations that revealed his thinking.

Understanding learning in bipolar dimensions as either knowledge transmission (as it was conceived by behaviourists) or knowledge construction (as it was understood by early constructivists) is a rather simplistic conceptualisation and interpretation of the complex nature of learning. Dewey (1997a:17) opposed the idea of conceptualising learning in terms of 'Either-Ors'. While he argued that knowledge of the past as *an end* of education may be rejected, its importance as *a means* to education cannot but be emphasised. For example, knowing theories for the sake of knowing them is not desirable; knowing theories in order to understand our past and current ways of life is what we are looking for in education. Dewey (1991:119) maintained that 'something must be already understood, the mind must be in possession of some meaning' in order to make thinking possible. Therefore, for personal experience (such as observations) to be extended into new learning, it must incorporate existing knowledge and other information.

Today, researchers take an integrated view of learning by acknowledging the importance of both 'learning *about* . . . and learning *how* . . .' (Kalantzis and Cope 2008:144). They consider existing knowledge and current experiences, formal and informal, as being dynamically interrelated to facilitate the process of thinking and make sense of studied phenomena. Vygotsky's (1978) socio-cultural theory, discussed next, provides a framework to understand the dynamic and complex nature of learning.

Vygotsky (1978) argued that learning is embedded in the particular social context (an idea already embraced by social learning theorists) with learners actively constructing their learning (a concept previously acknowledged by early constructivists). Vygotsky however emphasised (i) the dynamic interplay of individuals' activity with, and within, the activities of the community, where they live, work or study; (ii) the role of values, beliefs, customs and skills of that community; (iii) the mediating role of other knowledgeable people in the learning process; and (iv) the historical and cultural origins of the tools (such as language, observation etc.) used in constructing knowledge (Kozulin et al. 2003).

Theorist box 1.3

Lev Vygotsky

Lev Vygotsky (1896–1934) was an eminent Russian psychologist whose name is associated with the socio-cultural theory of learning. He understood and explained learning as a social activity that takes place through the social interactions with knowledgeable others. First, language and thought are interdependent, meaning that language contributes to thinking and thinking contributes to language development. Second, he emphasised the historical and cultural origins of the learning tools, and especially language, used by different societies. His ideas of the social and collective nature of learning and development were particularly influenced by the socio-political climate of Russia in his time. Vygotsky's books *Mind in Society: The Development of Higher Psychological Processes* (1978) and *Thought and Language* (1986) remain classic texts in the field.

Referring to children's learning, in particular, Vygotsky (1978) argued that, by participating in the activities of their community, children acquire and internalise 'spontaneous' concepts without any formal instruction. However, when they enter school, children are introduced to new ideas and specific methods of instruction. Through the assistance of knowledgeable others (e.g. teachers, peers or members of the community) children gradually make associations with, or combine, their prior 'spontaneous' concepts and skills with those introduced through formal instruction in order to reach a new level of learning. In Vygotsky's terms, we do not just learn facts and theories that are isolated and separate from the rest of our lives; we learn in relation to what we already know and in the light of our espoused values, beliefs and attitudes (Hein 1991).

Proponents of socio-cultural constructivism claim that learning takes place *in action*, as we participate in and reflect on the activities of our community, for instance our workplace, school or university. Learning in action, as is the case with learning by doing, requires the active involvement and engagement of the learner. However, learning *in action* is more than learning *by doing* (Hargreaves 2004). Whereas learning by doing is about the (re)discovery of ideas and principles already known, learning in action aims for the learner to reach new meanings and understandings on the basis of prior knowledge and personal experience. In essence, learning *in action* is about knowledge construction, whereas learning *by doing* is associated with the knowledge transmission model.

Observation – a learning tool

Socio-cultural constructivism offers a framework to understand the role of observation as a learning tool that provides learners with experience which is rooted in the particular context of the phenomena under study (e.g. child development, play etc.). Observation provides the basis for shared reflection with knowledgeable others in the field (e.g. peers, tutors and/or parents or practitioners, depending on where the observation has been conducted) and offers the opportunity to examine and re-examine previous knowledge, assumptions and understandings to reach new meanings that have currency among all those involved in the process.

In the light of socio-cultural constructivism, we see observation as a learning tool used in action to both *learn about* something (e.g. child development, play, teaching and learning practice etc.) and to *learn how we learn* (that is, to understand our own learning process). We see observation as a learning tool that has evolved over time and within the particular culture of childhood studies and practice (to be discussed in Chapters 2, 3 and 4) and it is used in the light of the values, beliefs and attitudes pertaining to that particular culture (to be explored in Chapters 5 and 7). It is a tool that is methodically and systematically used and rigorously reflected upon, analysed and interpreted (to be elaborated in Chapters 7, 8, 9, 10 and 11). It is a research tool that forms the basis for writing reflective accounts, reports and academic papers and it is used to inform everyday practice (Chapters 12, 13 and 14).

Summary

In this chapter, we have discussed observation as an everyday tool that equips us with insights and knowledge to make sense or our world. We then moved on to consider what learning is and the debates about knowledge transmission and knowledge construction and the uses of observation in the learning process. We concluded by adopting socio-cultural constructivism as our framework to understand the role of observation in learning as a knowledge construction process. Following this discussion, in the next chapter we will discuss how observation has evolved and developed over time in childhood studies and research.

Concluding activity

Consider some of the principles of knowledge construction, in the left-hand column of Table 1.1, and complete the right-hand column to indicate the implications of these principles for the uses of observation as a learning tool.

Table 1.1 Some learning principles – implications for observation

Learning principles	Implications for observation (to be completed)
Learning requires the active engagement of learners	
Learning takes place in social activities	
Learning happens through interaction with knowledgeable others	
Learning requires appropriate resources	
Learning is informed by existing knowledge and theories	

Chapter 2
Child observation – historical perspectives

In this chapter we discuss how observation has historically been used by key thinkers in disciplines related to education, and how it has been developed as a tool for child study. We start by discussing how scholars from disciplines such as biology, psychology and pedagogy used observation to study children. We then provide an overview of the key features and characteristics of their observations, signposting to uses of observation by contemporary researchers and some of the current debates about its use.

Vignette 2.1

During the first seven days various reflex actions, namely sneezing, hiccupping, yawning, stretching, and of course sucking and screaming, were well performed by my infant. On the seventh day, I touched the naked sole of his foot with a bit of paper, and he jerked it away, curling at the same time his toes, like a much older child when tickled. The perfection of these reflex movements shows that the extreme imperfection of the voluntary ones is not due to the state of the muscles or of the coordinating centres, but to that of the seat of the will. At this time, though so early, it seemed clear to me that a warm soft hand applied to his face excited a wish to suck. This must be considered as a reflex or an instinctive action, for it is impossible to believe that experience and association with the touch of his mother's breast could so soon have come into play.

Excerpt from Charles Darwin's observation (1877:285-6)

Vignette 2.2

18.6.25. The children let the rabbit out to run about the garden for the first time, to their great delight. They followed him about, stroked him, and talked about his fur, his shape, and his ways.

13.7.25. Some of the children called out that the rabbit was ill and dying. They found it in the summer house, hardly able to move. They were very sorry, and talked much about it. They shut it up in the hutch and gave it warm milk. Throughout the morning they kept looking at it; they thought it was getting better, and said it was 'not dying today'.

14.7.25. The rabbit had died in the night. Dan found it and said, 'It's dead - its tummy does not move up and down now.' Paul said, 'My daddy says that if we put it into water, it will get alive again.' Mrs I. said, 'Shall we do so and see?' They put it into a bath of water. Some of them said, 'It is alive.' Duncan said, 'If it floats, it's dead, and if it sinks, it's alive.' It floated on the surface. One of them said, 'It's alive because it's moving.' This was a circular movement, due to the currents in the water. Mrs I. therefore put in a small stick which also moved round and round, and they agreed that the stick was not alive. They then suggested that they should bury the rabbit, and all helped to dig a hole and bury it.

Excerpt from Susan Isaacs' observations (1930:182-3)

Introduction

The observations above provide evidence of how observation has been used over time by eminent scholars and theorists to study children. Bruce (1991) argues that awareness of historical influences can support thinking about present child observation. Within the socio-cultural approach to learning (discussed in Chapter 1), observation is understood as taking place within the context of what Daniels (2005:24) calls 'a historical legacy'.

While systematic observations in disciplines such as biology, physics and astronomy date from many centuries ago, observation as a systematic tool in studying children gained academic recognition only in the late seventeenth and eighteenth centuries. Although there is much historical evidence of informal diary records kept by mothers and other family members to document their children's development, it was the writings of early theorists such as John Locke, Jean-Jacques Rousseau and Pestalozzi that gave credence to child observation and by the nineteenth century child observation started to be systematically used to study children (Fawcett 1996).

In this chapter we discuss how key thinkers from disciplines such as biology, psychology and pedagogy used observation to study children, and provide an overview of the key features and characteristics of these observations. We will then consider the uses of observation by contemporary researchers and some of the current debates about its use.

The influence of biology

Early theorists, with a background in biology, have influenced the field of child study by using refined observation skills that they used in their own discipline. Biologists such as Darwin and, later on, Piaget used their observational skills to observe and record the development of their own children to arrive at conclusions about their development and thinking. Darwin's (1877) observations of his first-born son are the first record of systematic observation that gave credibility to the use of observations for the study of children (see Vignette 2.1).

Darwin's observations are of interest, not only in terms of the insight they provide about infants' development, but also about the kind and purpose of observation and the method of recording. Darwin claimed that he conducted *close observations* recording every detail and *wrote down at once* whatever he observed. From Vignette 2.1, however, we can see that he records more than he observes. He simultaneously recorded (i) what he observed; (ii) how he understood his observations in the light of what he already knew; and (iii) his emergent ideas and opinions about children. These are three distinct aspects of observation of which the observer should be aware and that may need to be recorded separately.

Theorist box 2.1

Charles Darwin

Charles Darwin (1809-1882), a British biologist, is best known for his theory of evolution, which explained the origins of life. Darwin used his acute powers of observation to study the flora and fauna in South America (mainly the Galápagos Islands) where he travelled on the *Beagle* in 1831. The differences and similarities of species in differing locations led him to postulate the idea of 'natural selection', whereby the best adapted creatures in a particular environment survive and reproduce, whereas others die out. He was also an eager child observer. He used his well-honed observational skills and analytic mind to observe all his ten children. He published the observations of his first-born son, where he hypothesised about child development. *The Origins of Species* (2006) is one of Darwin's well-known publications, while *A biographical sketch of an infant* (1877) refers to his child observation.

The influence of developmental psychology

At the end of nineteenth century, child observation was used by developmental psychologists to study children. Stanley Hall (1893; 1897a; 1897b) argued for the study of children in everyday environments such as home and school and he urged parents to maintain records of their children's development. He introduced the notion of naturalistic observations and highlighted their practical applicability. He used observations as the basis for providing appropriate educational experiences for children. He brought together developmental psychology and education by introducing child study into teacher training. Hall is credited as being the father of the child study movement. His views are still relevant and are echoed in contemporary early childhood researchers' arguments that child development knowledge is necessary for pedagogical effectiveness (Moyles et al. 2002).

In contrast to Hall's approach in using observation in children's natural environments and everyday activities, Gesell (1950) – a former student of Hall's – and his colleagues brought the children into a laboratory at the Yale Clinic of Child Development. They conducted the first ever large-scale study to examine the development of hundreds of children of different ages. Their particular contribution to observation was the development of highly sophisticated recording and monitoring methods such as one-way observation mirrors, photographic domes and cameras, which allowed them to observe children from all angles (Vasta et al. 1999). Although in a laboratory, Gesell observed naturally occurring behaviours that were not experimentally manipulated (Raban et al. 2003).

Gesell's contribution to observation was the introduction and use of innovative and advanced technical methods of conducting and recording observations. These methods allowed children's behaviours to be observed from different angles to gain a holistic overview and minimised the observer effect. Gesell corroborated his observational data using highly scientific methods. From his observations, Gesell concluded that there is a high degree of uniformity in children's development. Children do not develop at the same rate (e.g. some walked earlier than others), but the pattern of development was consistent (e.g. all children walk before they run, they run before they skip etc.). This work led him to establish statistical norms that documented the universal stages of children's acquisition of skills. Norms of child development continue to be a reference point for professionals working with children. Although, considering children's development against these norms remains a debatable issue, developmental screening is widely used by, for example, health visitors and other childhood professionals (Alexander 2002; Woodhead 1996; Working Group Against Racism in Children's Resources 1991).

The influence of behaviourism

During the early twentieth century, behaviourism influenced the way observations were conducted. Behaviourists adopted a highly scientific approach to observation, recommending the employment of rigorous and replicable methods such as those used by natural scientists. Skinner, for example, argued for *careful scientific* observations that focused on observable behaviours only, with the observers maintaining a detached approach (Skinner 1953). Observations were recorded as factual accounts of children's behaviour with no reference to contextual information and without making assumptions about what children may be thinking or feeling. Observers were advised to just 'keep to the facts' (Harding and Meldon-Smith 1996:41).

Today, much of the observational data collected by childcare and education students and practitioners is similar to the type of observation valued by behaviourists. Checklists, for instance, are widely used to collect factual data to monitor children's development and learning over a period of time, with observers taking a detached, non-participant perspective (Fawcett 2009). This kind of observation is perceived as having the advantage of providing measurable and accountable data, used for programme planning and provision for children.

The influence of psychodynamic theories

In complete contrast to behaviourism is the psychodynamic approach to observation that originates from Freud's theory of psychoanalysis. Esther Bick introduced the psychodynamic approach to observation for the training of psychotherapists and psychiatrists. She encouraged and supported her students 'to *see what is there to be seen* and not to look for what they think should be there' (cited by Reid 1997:1). Psychodynamic observations focus on understanding the unconscious mind and inner lives of babies and young children. The role of observer is to record not only the child's observable behaviour, but also to note what is happening in the setting of the observation and the observers' responses to observation. The purpose of the psychodynamic approach is to attribute meaning to the child's inner life, while considering contextual factors and the observer's own emotional state and responses to what is observed (Piontelli 1986).

This type of observation is often conducted in a family home. It involves weekly, one-hour visits to follow a baby's or very young child's development throughout a year (Rustin 2002; Miller et al. 1989; Piontelli 1986). Notes are not taken but very close attention is paid to the non-verbal signals of the infant and any interaction between the child and the adults present. A detailed account of the session is written up as soon as possible after the completion of the observation.

Psychodynamic observations have a distinct emotional quality. Some of the key features of these observations include: the very attentive role of the observer; an awareness of the effect of the observation process on both the observer and the observed; the emphasis upon the infant's feelings and emotions; and the use of the seminar group to discuss and explore the observations. Close psychodynamic observations require the development of the observer's sensitivity to capture and have an understanding of 'subtle, interpersonal, emotional dynamics as well as a deeper and broader view of behavioural phenomenon' (Piontelli 2002:10).

The influence of constructivism

Piaget, the founder of early constructivism, used naturalistic observation in combination with clinical interviewing and experimental manipulation in studying children (Piaget 2002; Piaget and Inhelder 1973). He observed children and he also questioned them about their responses and actions and, whenever appropriate, intentionally intervened to present obstacles and problematic situations to observe further their responses. Piaget's methods of observation were designed to explore the qualitative differences in children's thinking rather than the quantitative differences in their answers. He was particularly interested in understanding how children think and the reasons they give, especially when arriving at wrong conclusions, rather than what they know (Vasta et al. 1999). Piaget claimed that human beings are affected by the social environment as much as the physical; but his observations placed little emphasis on the social and cultural environments and their impact on children's learning.

The influence of early childhood pioneers

Montessori, an Italian pedagogue, has made significant contributions to observation and child study. She claimed that if a new and scientific pedagogy was to arise from the study of the individual, the method of observation should capture children's *spontaneous manifestations* without placing them under undue pressure and stress. Montessori argued that the observer should disassociate her/himself from *any preconception of any sort* about the observed children and methodically conduct and record observations. She claimed that a *preconception-free* approach to observation opens the door to great surprises and unexpected possibilities that children's spontaneous manifestations may demonstrate (Montessori 1912).

> ## Theorist box 2.2
>
> ### Maria Montessori
>
>
>
> Maria Montessori (1870-1952) was born in Italy and died in Holland, where she was exiled by Mussolini. Despite her parents' aspirations for her to become a teacher, Montessori studied medicine and, ironically, it was her professional engagement as a visiting doctor to institutions catering for children with disabilities that led her to acquire an interest in *scientific* pedagogy. From her observations during these visits she concluded that the development of children with disabilities was a pedagogical rather than medical problem. She noticed that children absorb knowledge almost effortlessly from their surroundings and she challenged the notion of normality and disability. Influenced by the work of Jean-Jacques Rousseau, Froebel and Pestalozzi and, on the basis of her systematic observations, she developed and published *The Montessori Method* (1912), which together with *The Absorbent Mind* (Montessori 1967) remain her well-known publications.

Montessori placed particular emphasis on the method of observation and the time and place for conducting them (Montessori 1912). Her approach to conducting observations into children's naturalistic environments and everyday activities gave credit to the importance of contextual factors, while her concern of not placing children under undue pressure shows her respect for children.

Margaret McMillan, a British nursery education pioneer, used child observations at her Open Air Nursery School in Deptford, London to maintain individual children's profiles. These profiles charted each child's achievements and progress according to certain preset categories such as:

> state of health; nervous system; sensibility to cold/heat; muscular control; automatic movements; walking and balance; power to wash; ability to dress; ability to run; ability to jump; sense of rhythm; ability to catch and throw a big ball; ability to eat; sense of touch, taste, smell, hearing; ability to sing; vision; speech; attention span; sensory perception; ability to make comparisons; behaviour in bath . . .
>
> (McMillan, cited in Moriarty 1998:55)

McMillan's form of record keeping presages individual child records, often incorporating checklists, which are maintained in many contemporary childcare settings.

Susan Isaacs, also a British educator, used observations to document children's activities in the experimental Malting House School in Cambridge, where she worked for three years. She and her assistants had collected quantities of rich observational records of children's regular activities, such as given in Vignette 2.2, to document and understand children's intellectual and emotional development. Isaacs was enthusiastic about Gesell's work and, like Stanley Hall, suggested that parents should keep journals recording their own children's progress in order to contribute to this scientific enquiry (Isaacs 1929). Being influenced by Freud and the psychoanalytic school of thought, Isaacs was also concerned that observations should capture 'the meaning of the child's experiences to himself' (Isaacs 1948: 84).

An overview of historical influences

At the beginning of the twentieth century, when psychology was introduced as a scientific discipline, child observation followed rigorous methods that mirrored those in the natural sciences. The observations were mostly laboratory-based, decontextualised, focusing on observable behaviours only, with observers remaining detached (e.g. Gesell, Skinner). Advances in understanding children's development in terms of its context and the work of early childhood pioneers challenged the *scientific* and *decontextualised* approach to child study. By the mid-twentieth century there was a gradual shift:

- from studying children in laboratories to studying children in naturalistic environments;

- from conducting context-free observations to observations that were contextually appropriate;

- from recording only the child's behaviours to recording the interactions between the child, her or his environment (both physical and social) and the observer responses;

- from observing and recording observable-only behaviours to attempting to capture the child's inner thoughts and emotional state;

- from the observer being distant and detached to being engaged and participating.

In reality, however, none of these dimensions are dichotomous, rather they represent a continuum shown in Figure 2.1.

Dimensions of observation	Continuum (Where we locate ourselves in this continuum depends on the purpose of observation)
1. Where do we observe?	Laboratory (for controlled behaviours) Naturalistic environment (for naturally occurring behaviours)
	▪ - ▪– ▪– ▪– –▪ –▪– –▪- –▪ - –▪ - –▪ - –▪ - ▪
2. What do we record?	Child's observable behaviour Child's observable behaviour & contextual information
	▪ - ▪– ▪– ▪– –▪ –▪- –▪- –▪ - –▪ - –▪ - –▪ - ▪
	Targeted behaviours All behaviours
	▪ - ▪– ▪– ▪– –▪ –▪- –▪- –▪ - –▪ - –▪ - –▪ - ▪
	Child's behaviour only Child's & observer's thoughts & feelings, & context
	▪ - ▪– ▪– ▪– –▪ –▪- –▪- –▪ - –▪ - –▪ - –▪ - ▪
	Context-free observations Context-bound observations
	▪ - ▪– ▪– ▪– –▪ –▪- –▪- –▪ - –▪ - –▪ - –▪ - ▪
3. What is the role of the observer?	Distant/detached (non-participant) Involved/engaged (participant)
	▪ - ▪– ▪– ▪– –▪ –▪- –▪- –▪ - –▪ - –▪ - –▪ - ▪

Figure 2.1 Dimensions of child observation and their continua

Polarised views of where and how we conduct and record observations, and whether we are detached or involved observers, are of limited practical use. In reality, the choice we make along these dimensions and their continua are guided and determined by the purpose of our observations. For example, if we choose to observe a child's patterns of interactions with other children in the nursery school, it is likely that we will observe the child in the naturalistic environment of the nursery school, record observable behaviours related to interactions only, without reference to contextual information, and we may choose a detached/non-participant role. If, on the other hand, we choose to understand how the child experiences these interactions and how it feels to be a child in these situations, we will still conduct the observations in the naturalistic environment of the nursery school, but our recordings will include contextual information alongside the child's behaviour and we may take a participant role.

The shifts in child study and the different ways of using observations are supported by Bronfenbrenner's (1979) ecological theory that explains child (and human) development in terms of the dynamic interrelationships between and within different systems in which the child finds her/himself (such as family, school etc.). Although the ecological theory did not directly address child observation as such, it provides a framework for conducting naturalistic observations, recording contextual information and the interactions between the child, the context (physical and social) and the observer.

Contemporary uses of child observation

Today child observation forms the basis of the work of many professionals, policy makers, researchers and students (Arnold 2003; Athey 1991). Professionals conduct observations for different reasons and with different aims depending on their professional capacity, role and responsibility. A practitioner working in a day nursery may observe the routine and activities of babies and young children in order to plan their care and learning. Health professionals observe in order to assess growth and development, to screen for disabilities and to make available appropriate provision. Similarly, other professionals use observations for specific professional practices and services. Researchers and policy makers use observations to address research questions that relate to different aims of their investigations to advance the field and/or inform policy. Students use observation to learn about, and acquire skills for, observation; to learn about the child and develop research skills; and to increase self-awareness about their own learning.

Child observation, however, has been criticised as a method used to classify children in relation to existing standards, such as norms of development or prescribed learning outcomes (Dahlberg et al. 1999). The observed child can be seen as a passive object under scientific scrutiny and without a voice (MacNaughton 2003; Woodhead et al. 1998). Others argue that closely observing children in their freely chosen activities is a way of listening to them and capturing their experience in a thoughtful and respectful way (Elfer 2005; Tudge and Hogan 2005; Nutbrown 1996).

Summary

It this chapter we have discussed how observation has been used by scholars from fields such as biology, child development, behaviourism, early constructivism, psychodynamic theories and early childhood. Clearly their own background and the conventions and trends of their own discipline influenced how they studied children and the way they used observation. The different uses of observation, however, have brought to the fore key issues and aspects of observation that are as relevant today as they were in their time. Currently a range of approaches and methods are available to professionals, policy makers and researchers, and students. We will discuss these in the next chapter.

Concluding activity

Return to Isaacs' observation in Vignette 2.2 to consider the type of observations she conducted. You may use the continuum and the dimensions in Figure 2.1 as a starting point.

Chapter 3
Methods of observation

In this chapter we discuss different methods of observation appropriate to different aims and questions posed by the observer. More specifically we outline some of the most frequently used methods of observation, discussing their strengths and limitations and exploring practical considerations. We conclude by arguing that methods of observation must be fit for purpose to address adequately the aims and questions of our observations.

Vignette 3.1

Terri, age 20 months, climbs down from the sofa and walks across the room to a puzzle and then sits down beside it on the floor. She holds a piece of her puzzle with her thumb and first two fingers. She puts the piece on the board and when it does not fit she rearranges it until it does fit. When it fits she shouts 'YAY' and claps.

Excerpt from an observation aiming to describe the child's motor skills

Vignette 3.2

John: Good morning what do you want?

Adult: Um, I like rabbits.

Billy: We don't have rabbits.

John: I know where they have got them . . . Sainsbury's [supermarket]. (There is a telephone on the 'shop counter'.)

Adult: Could you ring Sainsbury's to check if they have one for me?

John: Yes! (Starts dialling then pauses) Hello . . . Sainsbury's we have got somebody here who wants a rabbit . . . How much is the rabbit? (Looks at adult and says) £1.

Adult: £1 . . . Is that with the hutch?

John: Does it come with the hutch?'(Talks back on the telephone.) Yes it does.

Adult: If it's only £1 can I have two?

John: No, everybody has bought them.

Adult: Um, that's a shame.

John: But it is a really big one.

Excerpt from an audio-recorded observation, aiming to understand children's thinking through their use of language

Introduction

The two vignettes above show different ways of doing and recording observations. In the first, the observer appears detached from the situation and has chosen to record the child's motor skills in a narrative format. In the second vignette, the observer became a participant in children's play and audio-recorded their language and communication skills to understand the process of their thinking. In both situations, the observers could possibly have used different methods of doing and recording observations. What is crucial, however, is that you consider what it is that you want to find out through your observation and then choose an approach which will enable you to collect relevant information. Ultimately, the aim and questions posed for your observations will determine the methods you will be choosing (Hargreaves 2002).

In this chapter we outline some of the observation methods that are frequently used by professionals, researchers and students: checklists, time sampling, target child observations, sociograms, tracking maps, event sampling and narrative or running records and audio/visual recordings. Before doing so, we explore potential aims and questions posed for observations and consider their implications for choosing different methods of observation.

Aims of observation

As noted above, the observations in the two vignettes were conducted with different aims in mind. The first one was about describing *concrete observable* motor skills, while the second one focused on *understanding the process* of children's thinking through their language and communication skills. These are two different categories of aims that lead to different questions for our observations. The first category of aims is about *describing* factual information (e.g. types of behaviours and characteristics) and/or *measuring* and possibly *comparing* them. Some observations may be undertaken to examine initial hypotheses made about children's skills abilities, behaviour or learning. These aims relate to questions such as:

- What are the characteristics of young children attending an early years setting by gender, age, ethnicity etc. (e.g. description of each child's motor skills, as in Vignette 3.1)?

- How much, how many, how often or how frequently certain behaviours occur (requiring measurement).

- What is the difference or similarity between the characteristics of observed children by age, gender, ethnicity etc. (requiring comparison)?

- Do young children display more signs of anxiety in large groups than in small ones (exploring or testing a hypothesis)?

These questions usually require observations which provide numerical information or information that can be quantified. Some observation methods, such as checklists, time sampling, target child records, sociograms and tracking, may be more appropriate to use because they generate this form of data.

The second category of aims focuses on *understanding* and *meaning making* from the observed behaviours and characteristics or on *processes* that can explain them (as in Vignette 3.2). This category of aims poses questions such as:

- Why, for instance, child A prefers to play with child B, but s/he is isolated in large group activities? (focuses on understanding)

- How the daily routine supports children's learning across all curricula areas. (focuses on understanding and processes)

These questions require observations that provide in-depth and context-specific information. They need qualitative information about the observed child and the context, because the observed behaviours become meaningful only within a specific setting at a particular time. Narrative observations and, to some extent, event sampling are most appropriate for such questions. Qualitative data can also be collected via audio-recordings, photographs, video-recordings.

Of course the aims and questions of any observation may require both quantitative/numerical and qualitative/textual data. For this, some methods may be more appropriate than others or the observer may use more than one method. Thus, it is important that the observer: first, establishes the aims and questions for the observations; second, is aware of the range of methods available to choose from; and, third, feels confident in her/his skills in using them.

Different methods of observation

In the next section we outline eight methods of observation, these are: checklists; time sampling; target child observations; sociograms; tracking maps; event sampling; narrative observations; and audio- and visual-recordings. These methods are in common use and are also detailed elsewhere (see for example:

Fawcett 2009; Hobart and Frankel 2004; Sharman et al. 2004; Harding and Meldon-Smith 2002). We offer brief examples of their use, discuss their particular focus and the type of data they produce, outline some of their strengths and limitations, and suggest their appropriateness for different aims and questions posed for the observations.

Checklists

Checklists are useful when we want information about an individual child or a group of children and they are used when we mainly want to collect factual information that can be quantified, that is, summarised in numbers. When we complete a checklist we focus on the child's observable behaviour or actions only, without paying attention to or recording contextual information. Checklists are often used to monitor normative developmental progress or to record curriculum learning outcomes, using established and standardised checklists that are norm referenced or standardised, such as the Portage checklists, baseline tests on school entry, or other developmental checklists.

Observers may also construct their own checklist to observe aspects of a child's development or behaviour that might concern them. To construct your own checklist, you have to decide what information you want to gather (e.g behaviours and skills of a child or group of children). Then you itemise these skills or behaviours as statements in your checklist. Next, you have to decide what you want to record about these statements. Do you want to know whether they are present or absent, achieved or not achieved? If so you may construct a checklist, as shown below, that also leaves room for additional comments. Other checklists may be designed to measure the frequency by tallying or judging (e.g. 'Not at all', 'Sometimes', 'Often') the occurrence of specific behaviours or to rank the quality of identified statements (e.g. child's mathematical skills are: 'Limited', 'Good', 'Very good'). Once checklists have been devised and printed they are quite simple to complete, by ticking off when and if the behaviours occur.

Checklist excerpt, recording a child's social skills

Aspect of development:	Achievement	Comment:
Relates to adults	Y	Approached staff
Relates to peers	Y	Played with J, T and A
Helps with tidying	Y	Put Duplo® bricks in box

Key: Y = Yes; N = No; NS = Not Seen

Checklists may be completed once to have a snapshot of a child's or a group of children's progress at a particular time, or they may be completed repeatedly over a period of time to monitor change or progress. Checklists may show what a child can do, but they give limited additional information; the observer records only items that are on the checklist, whereas the child may display many skills that are not listed and therefore pass unrecorded. There is a concern that checklists may be constructed to record things that children cannot do, rather than their strengths and abilities (Bartholomew and Bruce 1993).

Time sampling

Time sampling is a method of observation that involves brief observations at set intervals over a period of time. For example, observe and record for two minutes every twenty minutes throughout a morning (see time sampling box below). These observations can collect open-ended data about the child, or preset behaviours can be used. The important feature of time sampling is that you devise a time schedule, stick rigidly to it and repeat it on at least one other occasion to ensure a holistic and consistent picture. As with the completion of the checklists, as an observer you maintain a detached stance and record only the observed behaviours.

Time sampling excerpt, carried out at a playgroup

09.10   Walks towards Adult 1 but stops at water tray and puts one hand in the water

09.30   Standing at the computer, looking at the screen, two other children are playing

09.50   Sitting on Adult 2's lap, looking at a book, head resting on the adult's shoulder

---

Some advantages of a time sampling method are that it offers a precise method of data collection through which perceptions about a child can be tested, for example 'Does she really always play alone?' or 'Is he constantly wandering around the room?' If there is a concern about a particular child, then this can be put into perspective. Time sampling offers snapshots of the child's behaviour, over a period of time, which when viewed in their totality may or may not substantiate initial concerns or hypotheses.

Time sampling can be challenging for the observer, who has to be alert and disciplined in order to record the samples at precise time intervals. If you are distracted by children or involved in another task, you may find maintaining regular time sampling difficult. Another disadvantage is that interesting, relevant behaviour may occur in between the sample times and so pass unrecorded. Time sampling is difficult to use simultaneously for a group of children, even if the same behaviours are observed.

Target child observations

Target child observations are used to collect detailed information about a child's experiences in a concise and structured manner, using an observation schedule prepared in advance. You need to identify codes that refer to the participants involved as well as the child, the different tasks and the context in which the task takes place (see excerpt below). It is essential to practise this method in advance to ensure that you can use the codes accurately and quickly, as you observe and record the happenings minute by minute and for as long as you decide to do so.

Target child excerpt

Time	Language	Task (in Music area)	Social group
13.45	TC → A 'Sing, sing!'	Mus	SG
13.46	TC → A 'sheep'	Mus	SG
13.47	TC + A + C + C 'Baa baa black sheep'	Mus	SG

Codes: TC = target child; A = adult; C = child; Mus = music; SG = small group

The advantage of this method is that it allows you to focus closely on the target child and record her/his observed behaviour (e.g. play, language, social interactions as excerpt above), to follow the sequence and flow of events, allowing the reader to visualise them like a video-recording. The method may present challenges as learning and applying the codes isn't always straightforward, and so using this method well requires practice and experience.

Sociograms

Sociograms are used to identify children's social interactions and friendship groups. They may be of particular use to test a perception that a particular child is isolated within a group, or in order to discover which children are popular with their peers. An observational sociogram can be created by following a particular child and recording her/his interactions, as in the excerpt below. A group of children can also be followed to create a sociogram of their interactions.

Sociogram excerpt, tracking a child's interactions

9.15   J → B and T

9.20   J + B and T

9.25   J and T

9.30   J and T + S

9.35   J → A (Adult)

Key: → moving towards or addressing another child/adult

+ denotes newcomer joining

A structured record of interactions may be useful to highlight one particular child's relationships or to consider social dynamics within a group. It could highlight a child's popularity, or reveal information about a child who has difficulty in making relationships. Sociograms provide only limited information; they may show who a child is playing with but do not reveal anything about the quality of the interactions; they may also prove unreliable, as young children's friendships change frequently and patterns of interaction may vary from day to day.

Tracking maps

Tracking maps, which are also referred to as trail or movement records, are used to discover how children make use of space and resources. Staff in early years settings may also use tracking maps to evaluate the activities provided for children. For this type of observation, you need to prepare a diagram, sketching the play area where you will be observing and code the various movements you record (e.g. starting and finishing point, moving between areas, playing in an area, watching other children in the area etc.). If you intend to create more than one record, you could photocopy the tracking map.

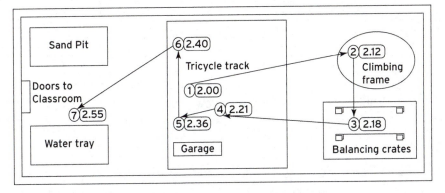

Figure 3.1 Tracking map, showing a child's use of the outdoor play facilities

There are then two main ways to use a tracking map. The first is to focus on an individual child or group of children to follow their movements around the play area, representing these as arrows and also noting timings, as shown in Figure 3.1. Tracking maps provide visual information about a child's choices of play activity and the amounts of time spent on different activities. The second way is to use tracking maps to create an overview of where all the children are playing at certain times, in order to establish how space and facilities are used. They can show which play opportunities children take advantage of and also which resources are popular and which are under used (Hargreaves 2002).

Tracking maps, however, only show the child's location of activity and not what he or she actually does. Like sociograms, a single observation may not be reliable and so several tracking maps would have to be completed to identify if play choices remain the same or are different. Tracking maps may be particularly useful when combined with other methods of observation.

Event sampling

Event samplings can be useful for recording particular occurrences, often of unwanted behaviour, in order to understand when and why they happen (see the boxed excerpt below). To conduct an event sampling observation, you need to spend time in the setting and be alert for instances of the events that you want to observe. As well as details of what the child does, you need to include contextual information and, if possible, what happens immediately before and after the event.

Excerpts from an event-sampling observation

Event 1:

10.10 (Baby Room, snack time, 2 adults, 5 children) Mary has finished her fruit, T and J are still eating theirs. Mary gets down from the table, walks towards J. He holds out his fruit to her and she bites his hand. He cries and she runs away.

Event 2:

15.25 (Baby Room, free play, 2 adults, 5 children) Mary is playing with the soft shapes, she's rolling around on the carpet, laughing. She goes towards T and starts to cuddle him, he screams loudly as she bites him. Mary looks and smiles.

Unlike time sampling, this method of observation provides event and context-specific information in addition to the child's observed behaviour. When reviewing event samples you can begin to understand more about certain behaviours, seeing patterns, and formulating alternative hypotheses to understand why they occur. The evidence can be useful as a basis for informed discussions about the child's progress or behaviour and for planning appropriate support, if required.

The major challenge in using this method is the identification of what constitutes an event. Another difficulty is that you may only start to record when you become aware that an event is actually happening and miss information about the antecedents prior to an event.

Narrative observations

Narrative observations, also known as running records, offer an opportunity to record a detailed account of a child's actions and contextual information, in an everyday situation. You record what is actually happening before your eyes, that is, what you are seeing and hearing, over a sustained period of time. You need to take notes during the observation which then are amplified soon after its completion to produce a narrative record that depicts what you have observed. Observers sometimes use audio- (as in Vignette 3.2) or video-recording to capture such detail. It is almost a contemporaneous record with as little time as possible elapsing between observation and recording, in order to capture accurately the details and the essence of the observation.

Close attention to a child over time may evoke thoughts and feelings in the observer. Taking account of these responses while observing is important, as your reactions to a child or a situation may influence what you see and what you record (an issue to be discussed further in Chapter 6) and later on your reflection and interpretation of your observations (to be discussed in Chapters 9 and 11, respectively).

It is important for the observer to be aware how these responses are recorded. The initial narrative recordings usually include details of the sensory data (that is, what we see and hear) and our responses as an observer (that is, our thoughts and feelings). Both are relevant in the analysis and interpretation of our observations (to be discussed in Chapter 11), but they need to be distinguished. One way of doing this is to record them in parallel (as shown in Figure 3.2). Elfer (2005) argues that it is very important for observers of young children to be sensitive to the complex emotions that may be evoked and to acknowledge the significance of feelings when carrying out and interpreting observations.

As an observer you may choose to be a detached/non-participant or a participant (to be discussed further in Chapter 7). Often, students are advised to

Observation record (Description of sensory information)	Reflections on observation (Observer's thoughts and feelings)
Anja is told off by the learning support assistant (LSA) for not listening. She is given more maths equipment and begins fiddling with it. After removing some cubes from the tray, she throws the others into the tray on the middle of the table. The LSA prompts her to write the answer on her sheet. The girl behind distracts Anja by calling out her name. The LSA asks her if she is ready. She squabbles over the equipment with another child. The LSA instructs her to put the equipment away. The teacher approaches the table looking disappointed. Anja laughs. Then she calls out the answer across the table. The LSA praises Anja and marks her answer. Anja is distracted by the child behind her again. They start chatting to each other. Anja stands up and pretends to dance.	During this observation, I soon felt frustrated and empathised with Anja. I felt that the LSA was not in tune with Anja. She did not support her adequately; instead she constantly instructed her what to do and she praised her, at times, when she could perhaps have withheld praise.

This was not a positive experience for Anja and I wanted to interfere. In hindsight my own feelings might have influenced how I have recorded this observation (e.g. Anja fiddling and squabbling over maths equipment; throwing them; the teacher instructing, prompting Anja). |

Figure 3.2 Narrative observation record form, distinguishing observable behaviours and the observer's initial thoughts and feelings

take a non-participant stance, as this gives them the time to concentrate on their observations. If however you want to get close to children and appreciate features of their lives, the complexities of their play and the ways in which they view the world around them, then you may choose a participant stance. In order to observe and understand the peer culture of children from a child's perspective, William Corsaro (1985; 2003), for example, developed a particular method of participant observation. He adopted an atypical adult role in activities in order to be accepted as a 'big kid' and playmate. From this position, being alongside children in their play and joining in when invited, he could observe their interactions.

Taking an atypical adult role and becoming accepted by children as a 'big kid' is not always simple. It is especially difficult to participate reactively in play without influencing or changing the children's behaviours. For example, having recorded the observation in Vignette 3.2, the observer was concerned that she had directed the play too much.

Audio/visual recordings

To capture detailed conversations, such as in Vignette 3.2, or record contextual information, observers often make use of technology, for example mobile phones with cameras and audio/video-recorders. Such media also allow observers to share their observations and reflect upon them with others and/or explore their feelings. Observers may also ask the observed children to use such media in order to appreciate children's perspectives (Webster 2010; Thompson 2008; Reed 2007).

While technology has opened new avenues in capturing detailed observations that otherwise it may not be possible to record, there are ethical and technical issues which need to be considered before such use. The use of technology and especially mobile phones, cameras and video-recording may be obtrusive, raise issues of anonymity and confidentiality (issues to be discussed in Chapter 5) and questions about who owns the photographs or audio and video files (the observed individual or the observer). Technology is also demanding and the observed individuals' awareness of its presence may lead to a stronger observer effect. In addition, there are also technical issues to be considered, e.g. competency in using the technology, deciding where to focus the camera or when to shoot, selecting perspective and angle. Analysis of video-recordings is also complex. While images can be revealing, Thompson (2008:9) argues that 'an image is not always a simple window to the world'. Instead it raises questions about reliability, validity and truthfulness arising from the meanings ascribed to the chosen images.

An overview of different methods of observation

Some methods of observing young children such as checklists, time sampling, target child observation, sociograms and tracking maps focus on accurate factual information related to the observed child or situation. They provide structured and systematic information recorded by an observer who maintains a detached and as neutral as possible a stance. The analysis of these observations usually yields data that can be quantified, for example calculating the amount of time spent on different activities or the frequency of occurrence of certain behaviours.

Other methods such as narrative observations, event sampling, and audio/video-recordings provide textual or visual information that capture both the child's behaviour and context-specific information. These records may lead to open-ended and unstructured information, recorded by observers who may either remain detached and distant from the observed child or situation or may choose to take a more participatory stance. Their analysis leads to qualitative conclusions such as key concepts and ideas around certain themes (to be discussed in Chapter 11).

The methods of observation discussed are often criticised as recording the child's observable behaviour only, without paying much attention to contextual information. They are often used to assess and classify the child's abilities in comparison with norms of child development or curricula outcomes. As such they may encourage a negative view of the child. Participant observations and event sampling, to some extent, are richer in information and content as they focus on both the child and the context. They offer observers valuable information for understanding what children can do in their particular environment or how the environment supports their development, learning and behaviour. Depending on the level of participation in the observed situation or activity, observers may also have the opportunity to gain glimpses and insights about the happenings through the eyes of the child.

This, however, does not mean that certain methods are better than others. The method chosen depends on the aims of your observation and the questions that these aims pose. Clearly, you will need to identify the aims and questions of your observations before conducting them.

Summary

In this chapter we have provided an overview of several methods of doing and recording observations. We have discussed their intended purpose, the way they are conducted and recorded, and their strengths and limitations. We concluded by arguing that their choice and use depends on the aims and questions posed for your intended observations. There is no particular method that is better than another; rather, methods of observation are developed to be fit for purpose. Therefore, when selecting which method to use, you should take into account the aims and questions posed for your observation and consider the strengths and limitations of the chosen method. Having decided on the methods to be used, you will next start planning your observations. The planning of your observations will be discussed in the next chapter.

Concluding activity

If you want to explore the question: *how outdoor play facilitates peer relationships and friendships,* what kind of observation methods would you use?

Chapter 4
Planning for child observation

In this chapter we discuss some of the questions you need to ask, and some of the decisions and practical arrangements you need to make in order to conduct your observations. We first discuss who you should observe, issues of access and decisions about selecting the observed child; we continue with where to observe and for how long; and we conclude with some guidance about maintaining reflective notes in addition to your observation records.

Vignette 4.1

A group of undergraduate childhood studies students are given the following assignment:

'Conduct a study of a young child's holistic development, based upon a series of observations, and write a 3000-word report discussing the growth of the child and your own learning.'

Vignette 4.2

When Ryan arrives to begin his observations at Rainbow Day Nursery he is told that the manager, with whom he made all the arrangements, is off sick and that there is no note of his visit in the diary. Ryan tries to explain who he is and why he is visiting but the staff are reluctant to let him into the nursery without authorisation.

Vignette 4.3

Sara is halfway through her study of two-year-old Jack when his family announce that they have exchanged their council house and are moving to another area to be closer to Jack's mother's family. Sara is very worried at first and thinks that her observations of Jack are wasted and that she will have to begin all over again studying another child.

Introduction

Clarifying the purpose of your observation will help you to make appropriate decisions and arrangements about who to observe, where, when and for how long. In this chapter each of these issues is discussed in turn. Equipped with this knowledge you should feel confident that conducting observations will be a positive experience for the children you observe, other individuals who are present during the observation (e.g. parents/carers, early years professionals, teachers) and yourself. This chapter is based upon our experiences of teaching about child observation and the questions that students have asked and some of the issues explored and discussed in seminar groups. We also draw upon the work of some other authors who have written about this topic (including Roberts-Holmes 2005; Harding and Meldon-Smith 2002; Cohen et al. 1997) although few existing texts give detailed advice.

Who to observe?

If you are carrying out observations to discuss a child's holistic development, as were the students in Vignette 4.1, you may decide to observe a child whose development is *typical* of her/his age. If you want and decide to observe the acquisition of gross motor skills you are likely to select a young child who is beginning to crawl or walk rather than an older child whose movements are already fluent and confidently coordinated. If you want to observe gender differences in play you will need to observe both boys and girls who are of the same age and share the same play environment and resources. If you want to observe how play is used in a nursery class to facilitate children's language and communication skills, you will need to conduct a series of observations of both structured and free-play activities. As a general rule, your overall aim and specific reasons for carrying out your observations will determine the child or group of children you choose to observe.

In order to achieve your aims practical issues, such as access to the child or children, are also important to consider. Your observations will be more likely to go according to plan if you can easily be accommodated within a setting. For example, you may choose a nursery or school used to supporting students and that has clear procedures in place to facilitate observational studies. There could be difficulties in maintaining access if, for instance, you choose to observe a child from a family who have a busy lifestyle and are often away from home. Similarly, if a child is ill and has frequent hospital appointments, it is likely to be inconvenient for that child to participate in your study. Despite a willingness to support you with your study, these and similar situations may lead to cancellation of agreed visits and interfere with your planned observations. There are also ethical dilemmas if a family feels under pressure to meet their commitment to you (this is discussed in Chapter 5). It is therefore important to think about these issues well in advance to ensure that your observations are conducted as required by your course of study or research project.

Questions of access disappear if you have your own children to study. There are strong precedents for this in the work of Darwin and Piaget (discussed in Chapter 2) and other studies by parents that have provided important insights into children's development (Bissex 1980; West 1972; Weir 1962). A close relationship with a child might provide you with a strong motivation to observe and your knowledge of a child's background and interests can promote fuller understanding of the meanings of her/his words and actions (Arnold 2003; 1999). If you are a family member or friend the child will be comfortable with your presence but may be surprised that you are busy scribbling notes rather than interacting with them.

Observing children who are well known to you may pose further difficulties and dilemmas. For example, there is a risk that you may produce biased observational accounts (to be discussed further in Chapter 6); or you may find it difficult, or be reluctant, to change your usual family role to that of an observer, especially if you aim to be a more detached, non-participant observer (to be discussed further in Chapter 7). Explaining to the child what you are doing may affect her/his behaviour, a phenomenon known as observer or Hawthorne effect (Roethlisberger and Dickson, 1939) (to be discussed further in Chapter 7). Whatever the circumstances, you will need to make an informed decision, weighing the advantages and disadvantages of your choices.

Access to a child, for study purposes, may be easier if you are employed in a setting. Your focus on any of the children in your workplace could provide important insights into their thoughts and feelings and enrich your relationship with them. In addition, as well as collecting information for your academic work, you may also be providing information for children's records. Again, as with observation of your own or a friend's children, alongside these advantages there are disadvantages. Observing a child in your setting may mean that you pay more attention to her/him and this may be perceived as preferential treatment, raising issues of ethics (see Chapter 5). You may also find that your child study requires more sustained time than you are able to give during your daily engagement with the children, leading to partial or fragmented information that may not meet the requirements of either your systematic observation and/or record keeping for children.

Selecting a child for observation

If you decide to observe a child, or children, within an early years setting, the next step is to identify an individual child to be observed. This decision may be left to you and you might use a method of random sampling (Gall et al. 2010), such as selecting the third child to enter through the nursery door or sticking a pin in the class list. Alternatively you might use purposive sampling

(Gall et al. 2010) relating to the aim of your observation. One such approach would be to engage in a discussion with professional practitioners, who may suggest a particular child. Or you may choose to observe a child who interests you, perhaps because they seem very involved in a specific activity or display skills that are relevant to your planned observations.

Whatever the method of selecting the child to be observed, it is important to consider its potential limitations and impact on your observation records. While, for instance, the random method is more likely to be unbiased, selecting a child because she/he has attracted your attention may lead to observer bias. Similarly, observing a child recommended by the professional practitioner and the background information given to you may also lead to biased records.

In addition to these issues, as a visiting observer you will need to engage in discussions with the professional practitioner, so that any records that are shared are treated and used with due caution. Your initial observation records may be decontextualised, partial and fragmented, lacking fine tuning and the sharp observational skills required for making judgements and decisions about children. Therefore your observational records should not be used for making formal assessments and judgements about the child's learning, behaviour and development (see Chapter 5).

Another choice to be made could be whether to observe just one child or to observe several; once again, your purpose for observing should guide you. If you want, for instance, to observe differences in three year olds' gross motor skills in play you will need to observe children who are of the same age and share the same play environment and resources. If you want to observe how activities are used in a nursery class to facilitate children's peer relationships, you may also need to conduct a series of observations that involve more than one child. Observing a group of children will provide you with interesting information about the focus of your observation, but it can also be challenging. Your attention will be constantly divided among the observed children, while you also need to consider ethical implications, such as how will you observe a group of children if you do not have all the children's assent and their parents' consent (see Chapter 5).

Where to observe?

Having chosen a child, the aims of your observations will largely influence how and what you observe (discussed in Chapter 3). These decisions will also determine where to observe; the place or places for observation need to be chosen so that you can get close to the child's experiences and observe the intended behaviour. For instance, if you are observing a child's holistic development over a period of time, as in Vignette 4.1, it is suggested that you should observe the child in different situations, so that you can notice how these environments offer possibilities for the child to develop, practise and demonstrate their skills. We now know that context is an important factor which impacts directly and indirectly upon children's development, learning and behaviour (Bronfenbrenner 1979).

Theorist box 4.1

Urie Bronfenbrenner

Urie Bronfenbrenner (1917-2005) was a world-renowned developmental psychologist, based at Cornell University in the USA. His work changed the focus of child study, from examining the skills and abilities of children, often in laboratory settings, to an analysis of the effects of context on growth and development. Bronfenbrenner's ecological systems theory, described in 1979 in his book *The Ecology of Human Development*, provides a model of environmental influences on development, often illustrated as concentric circles. The innermost circle, or microsystem, represents a context, such as a family or nursery, where the individual child may be studied. The next circle, or mesosystem, consists of interactions between the different microsystems in which a child is involved. The exosystem, surrounding this, reflects different social settings in which the child is not directly involved, but that are likely to have an impact upon his or her life (for example, parents' employers or local government agencies whose decisions affect the provision of leisure facilities). All these systems occur within a macrosystem, cultural, historical, political and economic circumstances, which influence attitudes and shape the social context. In more recent writings, Bronfenbrenner updated his theory to discuss how processes of human development occur, in interaction with the environment, throughout the life course.

Whatever the choice of place, it is important that it is a safe location, so that the observed child, and you yourself, feel secure and comfortable. This will safeguard the child's physical, psychological and emotional well-being, which is a principal ethical consideration (see Chapter 5). It will also allow you to take note of the relevant factors in the surroundings, as part of your observation.

Once you have selected a main place to observe, ensure that you find out about the local area. This could help you later to interpret your observational records in context, that is, to understand something of the circumstances in which the child is living, or being cared for and educated, and about the opportunities that may be on offer. This is particularly relevant for observations aiming towards a broad and in-depth understanding of a child (see Chapter 3). It is sometimes advisable that early observations consist of looking and listening, which enables you to familiarise yourself with the child and the context and spot potential opportunities for later observations. On the basis of the understandings you have gained, you could then plan further observations that relate to your over-all aim and focus upon topics of particular interest.

When to observe and for how long?

The aims of your observation will also determine its time and length. For instance if, for the purpose of your study, you use time sampling to understand a child's play patterns during the half-day s/he spends in a nursery class, then you will need to observe the child for the duration of this session. If you want to observe a child's play in the playground, then you will need to observe her/him during this time. Similarly, if you aim to study a child's holistic development through a series of observations (as in Vignette 4.1), you should consider varying the times at which you visit to observe.

The length of your observation will also be determined by the method of observation you use and the time spent at an early years setting or home. Observations have to be long enough for you to gain the required information. You could record a short but very detailed observation (for example, of a child using a pair of scissors) or a longer but more general observation (for example, of different choices of play equipment in the nursery garden).

Pre-observation arrangements

If you have taken account of the steps above, and have a clear understanding of what your observations will involve, you will be more confident to approach a child's parents or the leader of an early years setting to negotiate permission to observe. It will facilitate successful observations if you establish shared expectations of what you aim to achieve.

It is important that you approach the task of observing in a professional and flexible manner in order to maintain good relationships. If your initial contact with parents or the leader of the early years setting is informal, it is advisable to put your request in writing and receive consent for observation to avoid potential problems, such as the one experienced by Ryan in Vignette 4.2, above. Ryan, in this instance, felt disappointed, angry and very unwelcome, but he stayed calm and polite. He gave staff a copy of the letter that outlined his project and a photocopy of his Criminal Records Bureau enhanced disclosure form. The staff were reassured and offered him a date to visit the following week. Ryan agreed to this and, on the morning of this second visit, telephoned before he left home to check that the manager had returned and that he was expected. This second visit went smoothly and Ryan began to feel that his observations would succeed after all.

Sometimes, independently of how well you have planned your observations, you may still face unforeseen difficulty, such as that experienced by Sara in Vignette 4.3. If you face any difficulties or dilemmas during your study, view them as challenges that you need to overcome and learn from. You could discuss them with your tutors and fellow students, perhaps during reflective seminars (to be discussed further in Chapter 9); they may be able to offer suggestions and help you resolve your problems. For instance, after speaking to her friends and to her tutor, Sara began to see that there were other possibilities. She asked Jack's mother if she would introduce her to another parent with a child of a similar age. This worked well and Sara completed her observations by observing Aisha, who was also two years old. This made Sara's studies very interesting as she began to compare the two children and notice some similarities and differences.

Maintaining a Learning Diary

Throughout your observational study, you need to maintain a *Learning Diary*, by documenting reflective notes, methodological notes and theoretical notes. Reflective notes include a record of your initial feelings, thoughts, ideas, reactions and initial reflections about your observations (as suggested in Chapter 3, Figure 3.2). These types of notes will be taken into account for the interpretation of your observations (to be discussed in Chapter 11). You will also use these notes as background information to make judgements about your learning and personal development through your observational study.

Methodological notes focus on your pre-observation decisions and arrangements, for example: the aims of your observations; your method of observations; who you observe and why; what you observe; and why, where, when and for how long you observe. You need to sketch out a plan to cover the whole period of your observations. This plan needs to be flexible, so that it can be updated during your observations to include information and reflections about each observation as it is undertaken, including any difficulties that may arise, how you deal with them and possible consequences for your study.

The theoretical notes include summaries of reading that links with the particular focus of your observation, or reading associated with any issues which may come up during the observation. For example, if the focus of your observation is young children's development, you need to identify relevant textbooks, research articles and online resources and keep notes about what you read to inform the topic under study. These will be key references when you write about your observations (see Chapter 13).

Although we have separated these types of notes into three categories they are interrelated. For example, your personal reflections may influence the theory that you refer to and note; and your methodological decisions may be guided by your reading. The notes in your Learning Diary will be useful as, for critical discussion and interpretation of your observations, you will need to consider all three sources of information alongside your observation records (Figure 4.1). You will need to acknowledge how your conclusions from your observation records have been influenced by (i) your own feelings, motivations and responses, recorded in your reflective notes; (ii) the strengths and limitations of the tools you have used and the decisions you have made, recorded in methodological notes; and

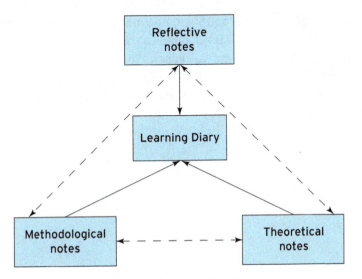

Figure 4.1 The interplay of the contents of the Learning Diary

(iii) the familiarity and understanding of existing literature in the field, included in theoretical notes.

Summary

In this chapter we have discussed some issues you need to consider and some questions to ask before you start your observations. In summary, the aim of your observation is the main factor to consider when deciding who to observe, where, and for how long. This has to be carefully balanced with practical and ethical concerns. Through reading this chapter, you have probably begun to realise that child observation is a complex task that requires good planning and organisation skills. You will also need to foresee and anticipate any potential difficulties and challenges and consider ways of addressing them. You will need to approach your observation with a professional attitude and manner, in order that the children, their families and/or carers have a positive experience which contributes to understanding the children's learning, development and behaviour, as well as informing your own learning and/or professional practice.

Concluding activity

Take some time to think about issues that might be raised when you select a child to observe. Some of the options below have already been mentioned in this chapter, while for others you will need to think about your own responses. Consider some positive and negative reasons for observing each of the following children: a child suggested by staff; a child who is completely unknown to you; a child with additional support needs; or a child for whom English is not their home language.

Chapter 5
Ethical implications of child observation

In this chapter we discuss the ethical implication of conducting observations and outline some of the issues you should consider before you request access to a child and/or setting. We first provide an overview of ethics in social sciences and research, and then discuss the requirements to gain informed consent from both adults and the child to be observed. We address some of the dilemmas experienced by observers and conclude with the fundamental principles of safeguarding children's well-being.

Vignette 5.1

For his final year major project, Gavin decided to investigate the language acquisition of young children who recently arrived from another country and do not speak English. The head teacher of the local nursery school has happily agreed for Gavin to observe Troy, four years old, who was enrolled last month. The head teacher said that parental consent was not necessary, as the head teachers operate in loco parentis. *Anyway, Troy's parents do not speak English, so it is unlikely that they will read the letter. Gavin had some hesitations about this arrangement, but thinking that he might not be able to find such a level of cooperation from another nursery school, he opted to act upon the head teacher's suggestions.*

Vignette 5.2

As part of her studies, Annie plans to study the play of boys – two to three years old – in day care. She will be conducting a series of observations of four boys over a period of three months. Annie approached the person in charge of the local day care unit to ask for permission to conduct her observations there. No objection was raised, but it was suggested that she seeks parental consent for all four boys, before starting the observations. Three parents provided written consent. The fourth parent (the mother) said that she had no objection to her son being observed as long as he is happy to be observed. Annie is wondering how she will receive consent from a three-year-old child; would it be better for her to chose another child? By doing so, however, she feels that the start of her observations will be delayed further; she is already one week behind schedule.

Vignette 5.3

As part of the module 'The Developing Child', Maria is required to conduct a series of observations. She made arrangements to observe Tim Coles, three years old, who at the age of two was identified as displaying developmental delay. Tim's mother, Annette, does not agree. Maria explained to her tutor that she does not need informed consent. She knows Annette very well; she is her fiancé's sister. In addition, this observation is a mutually convenient arrangement. Annette hopes to use Maria's observations to convince the health visitor that there is no developmental delay.

(Tim Coles and Annette are pseudonyms but Maria used the real names, when she discussed her observation planning in a seminar.)

Introduction

Accessing a child may seem to be a straightforward process but, as the vignettes above show, there are many issues about which you should think before you start your observations. An essential requirement is that you receive *informed consent,* that is, the permission to conduct the observations, but not everyone agrees whose consent is required. For example in Vignettes 5.1 and 5.2, there is a discrepancy of opinion as to whether the practitioners' consent was sufficient or whether the students needed parental and/or the child's consent. Vignette 5.3 raises additional issues such as anonymity, whether consent is needed if observing in a family situation and whether the student's observational data is appropriate to be used for professional judgements.

In this chapter we discuss some of the ethical implications of child observation by discussing briefly the role of ethics in social sciences and offering guidelines for informed consent requirements. We then outline the observers' responsibilities for safeguarding participants' well-being and ensuring quality observations.

Ethics in social sciences and research

The field of ethics originates from the Hippocratic Oath in antiquity (fifth century BC), but it was the Nuremberg War Trials and, later, the World Medical Association Declaration of Helsinki, that set out the current principles and standards for research involving human participants (The Nuremberg Code 1947; The WMA Declaration of Helsinki 1964/2008). Ethics in social research, however, is a recent phenomenon that has attracted particular attention during the last three decades. Social researchers now acknowledge that although their research may not physically harm or kill their participants, it may still have unintended psychological and social effects such as unwarranted anxiety, embarrassment, feelings of being excluded and betrayed, and/or creating false expectations and promises. Social research also has implications for and raises questions about issues of power and dominant voices, especially in research that involves marginal and vulnerable populations (e.g. young children, groups from different cultures, race, ethnicity, social class, gender and religion etc.), and the impact of the findings on these groups (e.g. stigmatisation, marginalisation, disaffection etc.) (Alderson 2004).

Theory box 5.1

Excerpt from The Nuremberg Code

The voluntary consent of the human subject is absolutely essential. This means that the person involved should have legal capacity to give consent; should be so situated as to be able to exercise free power of choice, without the intervention of any element of force, fraud, deceit, duress, overreaching, or other ulterior form of constraint or coercion; and should have sufficient knowledge and comprehension of the elements of the subject matter involved as to enable him to make an understanding and enlightened decision . . . The duty and responsibility for ascertaining the quality of the consent rests upon each individual who initiates, directs or engages in the experiment. It is a personal duty and responsibility which may not be delegated to another with impunity . . .

The Nuremberg Code (1947)

Many professional and research organisations have now developed appropriate guidelines. For example, the British Educational Research Association (BERA 2004) produced the *Revised Ethical Guidelines for Educational Research*, while the Economic and Social Research Council (ESRC 2010) introduced the *Research Ethics Framework* for social researchers. The National Association for the Education of Young Children in the States (NAEYC 2005) also drafted the *Code of Ethical Conduct and Statement of Commitment*.

Theory box 5.2

Excerpt from the NAEYC *Code of Ethical Conduct and Statement of Commitment*

NAEYC recognizes that those who work with young children face many daily decisions that have moral and ethical implications . . .

The Code sets forth a framework of professional responsibilities in four sections. Each section addresses an area of professional relationships: (1) with children, (2) with families, (3) among colleagues, and (4) with the community and society. Each section includes an introduction to the primary responsibilities of the early childhood practitioner in that context. The introduction is followed by a set of ideals (I) that reflect exemplary professional practice and by a set of principles (P) describing practices that are required, prohibited, or permitted.

The **ideals** reflect the aspirations of practitioners. The **principles** guide conduct and assist practitioners in resolving ethical dilemmas.* Both ideals and principles are intended to direct practitioners to those questions which, when responsibly answered, can provide the basis for conscientious decision making.

*There is not necessarily a corresponding principle for each ideal.

NAEYC (2005:1)

Awareness of the ethical implications of social research has also been the force behind the establishment of university research ethics committees, which provide information about institutional procedures for researchers and students to receive ethics approval to proceed with their studies. These procedures and guidelines aim to provide safeguards for all those involved in research, be it the participants, researchers or those who are peripherally involved such as gatekeepers.

The UN Convention on the Rights of the Child (1989) has been a hallmark in changing how research with children is conducted by acknowledging children as being full human beings with rights. Every child is seen as important, independently of her/his abilities, origins and gender and her/his views and opinions are significant. The acknowledgement of children's right to voice their views on matters that affect them has laid the foundations of exploring the ethical principles of doing research with children.

Informed consent and participant information

Participants' voluntary consent is absolutely essential in research (see excerpt from The Nuremberg Code 1947, above) and this principle is equally important for your observations. Independently of your status and relationship with parents and professionals involved, you should always ask for and receive written informed consent. If family relationships and friendships are involved, it is equally, if not more, important to receive informed consent to avoid jeopardising these relationships. If you are a professional or practitioner who conducts observations as part of regular duties and responsibilities and you want to use them for your studies and/or publications, you will need to receive informed consent from your participants and the adults in charge. There should be a clear distinction between your professional role and your role as student or researcher.

To receive informed consent you will need to provide appropriate information to ascertain the quality of consent received. The more information you provide the more likely it is for parents and gatekeepers to make an informed decision about your observations and decide whether or not to consent (Greig et al 2007; Morrow 2005; Alderson 2004; Bell and Nutt 2003; Coady 2001). The information provided is known as *participant information*, usually presented in a letter that should include the following information:

- *Who you are*. Your name may first come to mind, but further information is also necessary, for instance your status as a student; your institution and programme of study. Usually, this information is further confirmed by an institutional letter, written by the module tutor or programme leader. You will also need to attach a copy of your Criminal Record Bureau (CRB) clearance and contact details for further communication.

- *The purpose of your observation*. Explain the aim of your observation clearly. State, for instance, whether you will be looking at a specific aspect of development, or overall development, behaviour, interactions etc. This information will help you and parents/teachers to decide the appropriate context and times for your observations.

- *The importance and value of your observation*. It is unlikely that your observations will have a direct impact and practical value for the child her/himself. Highlight however the importance of your observations for your own learning and the development of your knowledge and skills as a future professional practitioner. Clarify that your observations will not be used to make any judgements about the child, as this is a learning exercise not a professional activity. This will help you to avoid the situation which Maria is experiencing in Vignette 5.3.

- *Details of a practical nature*. Indicate how many observations you want to conduct, for how long, where and who might be present; whether you would like to have permission to take any photos or to tape/video-record the child's conversation and actions.

- *Information about audio/video-recordings and photographs*. Explain how photographs will be used, for example in seminar presentations, dissertations that may be publicly available in the university library, in paper publications and/or books. You will need to receive consent for each level of use, and for the exact period of storage and use. Clarify who owns the photographs and include a relevant clause in the informed consent form.

- *Information about the use of observational records*. Explain whether the observations are for discussions with peers and tutors, your final assessment and/or publications, if appropriate.

- *Information about anonymity and confidentiality.* Explain that you will use pseudonyms and you will not include details that may lead to deductive inference. Often, although actual names are not used, other information may lead to identification of the child, his/her family or the early years setting. Point out that photographic evidence compromises anonymity to the agreed level of consent.

- *Child protection issues.* Explain that child protection issues will supersede the agreement for confidentiality, if the observations raise concern about malpractice and the child's well-being. You will reserve the right to follow the statutory procedures.

- *Potential risks to the child.* Explain how you will deal with situations where a child may become upset, withdrawn or feel pressurised to perform and reassure your participants that you will suspend observations, if necessary.

- *Inform parents and gatekeepers of their right to ask any questions* at any time before and during the observation and of their right to withdraw consent at any time for any reason, if they wish to do so.

- *Use of observational records.* Explain how you will be using the observations (e.g. in seminar discussions, assignments, research projects or published papers). Reiterate that, in your capacity as a student, you will not use them to make any judgements or offer a professional opinion about the child's development, learning, behaviour or progress.

- *Debriefing.* Explain how you will debrief your participants and whether you will give parents and gatekeepers copies of your observational records. If so, you need to state that these are learning materials that carry little significance for making any judgements and evaluations. These clauses may not apply if you are a practitioner in the early years setting.

(For an exemplar of a participant information letter, see Appendix 1.)

You will also need to consider procedural issues such as:

- *Keeping the participant information simple, concise, and avoiding long and wordy letters with unfamiliar terminology.* If necessary explain verbally any points that lack clarity.

- *Requesting two signed copies of informed consent from parents/gatekeepers and/or the child.* Give them a copy and file one for your records.

- *Keeping a copy of both the participant information letter and the signed informed consent for your records.* The tutors may request you include them as part of the work you submit for assessment.

Seeking the child's assent

The Nuremberg Code (1947) has made informed consent mandatory, but its statement that 'the person involved should have legal capacity to give consent' has left children and young people outside of this requirement. As a result, for many years parents' and gatekeepers' consent has been considered an adequate provision. Alderson (2004) points out that, for a long time, children have been *unknowing subjects,* but she acknowledges that as our values have changed so has their status; children now are seen as *aware subjects* and *active participants* who may influence processes that relate to their lives and experiences. The UN Convention on the Rights of the Child (1989) has changed the landscape by stating that:

> The child shall have the right to freedom of expression; this right shall include freedom to seek, receive and impart information and ideas of all kinds, regardless of frontiers, either orally, in writing or in print, in the form of art, or through any other media of the child's choice.
>
> (Article 13.1)

Considering, again, the question of whether or not you need informed consent from children, we can certainly say yes, if we are to exercise the Rights of the Child. However, from birth to eighteen years of age (the definition of the child in terms of her/his chronological age) there is a wide range and different levels of abilities, capabilities and maturity. For example, you may be able to provide written participant information to and receive written informed consent from a ten-year-old child, but this would not be appropriate for a young child of three, four or five years old. For the latter group of children you will need to use alternative means of communication (e.g. pictures, photos, drawings, maps, diagrams, videos) to explain who you are, what you want to do and how you will be using your observations.

In general, when you provide information to children you should reassure them, as you would with adults, of the following:

- If they do not like being observed, they do not need to agree.

- If they have agreed to be observed, you will still ask them again every time you do so. This is a process known as receiving the child's assent rather than the one-off consent that is required from adults.

- You have spoken to their parents and they have agreed to the observation, but explain that the child can still refuse to be observed.

- You will discuss the observations with your teacher/tutor to learn more about children and you may share these observations with them, the child's parents and teachers.

- Photographs will be taken only if the children and their parents agree to this.

Further ethical dilemmas

Seeking the child's consent may mean the child becomes aware of being observed and thus changes her/his behaviour (the *Observer* or *Hawthorne Effect* discussed in Chapter 7). There may be a temptation either not to seek informed consent from the child or to conduct covert observations in order to record what is perceived to be objective and naturally occuring behaviours. There is no single answer with regard to children's awareness of being observed. In general, how children are treated, in the observational process and in any research, is determined by balancing three basic principles, which are:

1. *The Rights of the Child*, which require that children are informed and facilitated to express and voice their views and opinions.

2. *Proportionality*, which requires a balance between the potential harms and benefits of conducting your observations.

3. *Doing good*, which requires that research and, in effect, observations, should do good to its participants and does not disadvantage anyone else. (Alderson 2004; The Nuremberg Code 1947).

Still this is not a simple and straightforward process. For example, you may argue that, even though your observation does not benefit directly the child her/himself, it contributes to your own learning and knowledge, which in turn you will use with other children in the future; thus *doing good* indirectly. Similarly, you may argue that observation is a low-risk activity that does not place the child at any risk, thus there is no need to ask her/his consent.

Weighing these arguments, different students or researchers may come to different decisions depending on their ethical stance, their values and principles. There is no single answer applicable to all cases and often one answer raises further dilemmas and questions. For example, by not asking for informed consent because the child is not placed in any danger, do you ascertain that the quality of your observations is more important than upholding Human Rights values (i.e., seeking informed consent)? Similarly, if Human Rights values prevail, would there be an adverse effect or restriction on your observational data?

Of course the tendency may be to follow one or the other option, but the actual answer comes from the effort to balance the two and this is a fine balancing act. It requires a high level of alertness and constant questioning of our own values, beliefs and ideals, or other people's beliefs and attitudes that may be unquestionably accepted, or beliefs and values that represent dominant and powerful voices. An ethical stance to your work requires that you are constantly posing questions such as: Why do I decide what I decide? And, what do my decisions say about my beliefs and values? Such questions will substantiate your principles and inform your practice.

Fundamental principles

While you will experience many ethical dilemmas in preparing and conducting your observations, and support will be available via the discussions with your tutors and fellow students, there are certain principles that you should always adhere to. These include (Alderson 2004; Coady 2001):

- *Anonymity.* You will not use the real names of the observed child, her/his family, the early years setting or any information that may lead to deductive inference.

- *Confidentiality.* All information is confidential and you will not disclose it, unless there are child protection implications. You disclose your concerns only to appropriate people who will guide you on how to deal with the situation.

- *Privacy and non-intrusiveness.* It is important that your presence is not intrusive. You will schedule your observations at times that are convenient for the child, family or early years setting.

- *Avoiding risks.* You will make arrangements to observe the child in the presence of another responsible adult. You will not attempt to prepare tasks to test theories and ideas.

- *Honesty.* You will avoid deception by clearly stating the purpose of your observations and your lack of professional status to arrive at any conclusions, especially when such expectations are raised.

- *Respect for children.* You will use age-appropriate language, when communicating with the children, and avoid using language that reflects certain assumptions and stereotypes about children.

- *Cultural awareness and respect.* It is essential that you are culturally aware and show respect for the ways people from other cultures behave and do things. Be mindful that there is not only one way of doing things, as there is not always one way of being and doing good.

Ethics: the basis for quality observations

Adhering to ethical issues is not just a procedural matter; instead it allows you to think and clarify in your mind what you want to do, how and when. Involved parents/professionals and the child need to have a clear idea of what they are agreeing to. It makes communication open and collaboration straightforward. It minimises the chances of experiencing potential unforeseen difficulties (e.g. withdrawal of consent, requests for using observational information for purposes other than your own study). In general, making available appropriate information means that the informed consent received is voluntary and free of misunderstandings and deception (The Nuremberg Code 1947).

Summary

In this chapter we have discussed the ethical considerations and requirements in conducting observations with young children, such as providing participant information and seeking adults' informed consent and the child's continuous assent. We have addressed some of the continuing dilemmas about observation ethics and highlighted the importance of the observer's alertness and awareness of the need to balance ethical principles to conduct sound ethical observations that demonstrate an ethical stance.

Concluding activity

Considering Vignette 5.2, devise an appropriate participant information letter and an assent form to be used with the children to be observed.

Chapter 6
Finding the role of the observer

In this chapter we discuss observation as a product of perception that is influenced by the observer's attitudes, expectations and emotional states. We explore the relevance of different social psychological theories to understanding and appreciating the complex mental processes that take place during observation. It is important for the observer to recognise the influence of these processes on the observation and, thus, seek to increase self-awareness.

Vignette 6.1

Annie is sitting among other children in the carpet area. She is well dressed, in fashionable jeans and a pretty white top. She has her legs crossed and her arms rest on her lap. She listens to the teacher attentively, smiling from time to time. Anytime the teacher asks a question, Annie holds her arm up. The teacher did not ask her to answer any questions. I am wondering why; she is such a well-mannered and well-behaved child (I wish all the children in my class behaved like this). Annie seems disappointed, but she is still smiling.

Annie moved to a table with three other children. They chat and draw pictures. Annie tried to reach the case with the coloured pens. One of the boys quickly grabbed it and put it in front of him, covering it with his arms and body and staring at her in a mischievous way. Annie suddenly threw her picture and pens on to the boy and the other two children. She stood up and walked away. I was surprised by her outburst. She seemed to be so well behaved and confident. (I suppose there is a limit to how much one can put up with.)

Vignette 6.2

Annie is sitting in the carpet area with the rest of the children (approximately 20). The teacher has just read a story and she asks the children questions. Some children shout the answers out while they hold their hands up. The teacher ignores the answers and asks individual children to respond. Everytime the teacher asks a question Annie holds her arm up, shaking it vigorously to be noticed. Two boys are sitting next to her and shout out the answers before the teacher asks them to do so. A few times, Annie turned around and looked at them very seriously, saying something. (I think she tells them not to do so. Annie is well behaved, but it seems to me that she is too eager to please, as I was as a child. She conforms to the rules, but I am wondering whether the teacher noticed her.)

> ## Vignette 6.3
>
> *Mrs Crisp is an excellent, warm-hearted teacher, in whose class children learn well. She has been in the school for over thirty years and is now teaching children whose parents were once in her class. Most parents are impressed by the bright, cheerful atmosphere of her classroom and the equipment and resources available to encourage the children to learn . . .*
>
> *A class of five-year-old pupils are changing their clothes for a physical education lesson. One child, John, carefully removes each garment and folds it neatly. He is the last child to be ready. Mrs Crisp speaks sharply: 'Hurry up John, no need to fold things just like your father in the menswear shop.' I was surprised to hear this remark from Mrs Crisp. It was really a derogatory remark. I didn't expect it.*

Introduction

Vignettes 6.1 and 6.2 show that, although the two observers viewed the same event, they arrived at different conclusions about Annie's behaviour. The first observer perceived her as being *well mannered* and *well behaved*, while the second concluded that she is *compliant* and *too eager* to please. In addition, the observer in Vignette 6.1 used her first impressions of Annie to interpret her behaviour in the subsequent incident. Similarly, in Vignette 6.3, the observer's first impressions of Mrs Crisp, based on previous knowledge about her reputation, created expectations that did not match the observation.

When we conduct observations we may attribute to our observed children or adults characteristics that are not directly observable. We may infer them from contextual information and cues or we may construct them in the light of our own attitudes, expectations, past knowledge and experience (Shaver 1987; Pennington 1986; Cook 1979; Tagiuri 1969; Bruner and Tagiuri 1954). This is illustrated across all three vignettes above, where it appears that the observers' own attitudes, expectations and feelings have influenced what they observed and the meaning they gave to their observations. As a result the observational records are a mixture of sensory data and their immediate interpretation. Awareness of the role of attitudes, expectations and feelings on the observational process will help self-reflection and ability to distinguish between what we actually see and what we infer.

In this chapter we explore the role of attitudes and how they may impact or interfere with the process of perceiving and interpreting information. We also discuss the roles of first impressions and incongruent information, categorisation and stereotyping, prior experience and emotional states to illuminate the process of observation.

The role of attitudes

Allport (1973:22) claimed that 'Attitudes determine for each individual what he will see and hear, what he will think and what he will do.' At one level, attitudes serve as the observer's lenses, prompting selective attention to certain characteristics and information while ignoring or dismissing others, leading to *perceptual bias*. At another level, attitudes form the basis on which observers make simultaneous judgements and evaluations about the perceived individual or situation, leading to *inferential bias* (Stahlberg and Frey 1988; Sherif and Hovland 1961).

For example, if we observe a child who we find attractive, as in Vignette 6.1, we may then focus on and record selectively information that is associated with attractiveness (e.g. being well dressed, wearing fashionable jeans and a pretty white top etc.). This is the process of perceptual bias. We may also interpret the child's behaviour in positive ways (e.g. being well mannered and well behaved). In addition, we may use these initial evaluations to explain subsequent behaviours, although these may contradict our initial evaluations (e.g. the observer making the point that she was surprised by Annie's outburst, but s/he was able to justify it). This is the inferential process of observation.

The perceptual and inferential processes take place simultaneously. They interact with each other to influence our perception of what we see and hear and our inferences or judgements from sensory data. Our initial observation record is usually an amalgam of these processes (see Figure 6.1) that need to be untangled (as we suggested in Chapter 3).

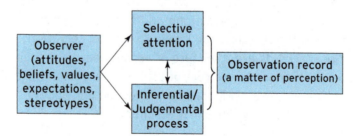

Figure 6.1 The perceptual process of observation

These processes can be understood in the light of congruity and dissonance theories, which assert that individuals strive to achieve cognitive congruity and consonance between what they know and believe and what they see and do (Festinger 1957, see Theory box 6.1; Osgood and Tannenbaum 1955, see Theory box 6.2). This means that, in the name of a balanced state of mind, observers may shape data and information to fit their preconceived ideas.

Theory box 6.1

Dissonance theory

Dissonance theory claims that individuals strive towards consistency between what they know or believe and what they do by reconciling contradictions. When individuals are in a state of dissonance they experience a pressure to reach a state of consonance either by trying to seek and select attitude-relevant information or by reordering, or adjusting, their current perceptions and/or previous knowledge. Individuals' commitment to their own attitudes produces a strong selective effect towards seeking information that is relevant and close to their own attitudes. In contrast, individuals who are not committed to their attitudes are open to any new information that may result in attitude change. As a result, individuals who have strong attitudes either integrate or argue against dissonant information, while individuals with relatively weak attitudes tend to change their viewpoint when faced with new, dissonant information.

Festinger (1957)

Theory box 6.2

Congruity theory

According to congruity theory individuals tend to see and perceive stimuli in a bipolar manner and in terms of pairs of opposites (e.g. good-bad; strong-weak; beautiful-ugly; active-passive and so on). Having perceived someone as being good, then, individuals tend, first, to attend to characteristics that confirm this initial perception and, second, to use this original perception to attribute associated characteristics in order to maintain congruity between existing perception and new information. This is particularly so when people hold strong and

▶

intense attitudes that are resistant to change. Less rigid attitudes allow people to absorb more information across the continuum of bipolar opposites rather than at their extreme opposite ends.

Osgood and Tannenbaum (1955)

The impression formation theory is also helpful in understanding psychological processes that take place during observation (see Theory box 6.3). This theory maintains that first-noticed characteristics form a lasting impression into which we fit and adjust characteristics observed later, in order to maintain the stability of that first impression. This might have been the case in Vignette 6.1 where, the observer having formed a positive first impression of Annie, s/he adjusted later information to fit and maintain this first impression. Similarly, in Vignette 6.3, having formed an initial positive impression of Mrs Crisp the observer expected similar positive behaviour; the actual observation however brought her/him into a dissonant state of mind that needed to be reconciled.

Theory box 6.3

Impression formation theory

The impression formation theory argues that the impressions individuals form of other people are a dynamic product of all the information they receive and that the overall impression formed is greater than the sum of the parts. However, there are certain personality traits that are more important than others in the final impression, because they allow for other inferences and connotations to be made.

Furthermore, it is not only the information individuals receive about other people that is important. The order in which individuals encounter such information makes a considerable difference in the impressions they form. It is a common belief, confirmed by psychological research, that first impressions are lasting, carry more weight and have more influence (primary effect) over impressions formed later (recency effect). There are three explanations for the primary effect phenomenon: (i) later information is interpreted in relation to information first received; (ii) later information takes less attention due to fatigue or boredom; and (iii) later information is discounted because it is in contrast with what came earlier.

Ash (1952)

The impression formation theory also maintains that some characteristics are more salient than others in forming a first impression. For instance, consider the following lists of words and think about the individuals each describes:

1. A is a warm, intelligent, skilful, industrious, determined student.

2. B is a cold, intelligent, skilful, industrious, determined student.

3. C is a polite, intelligent, skilful, industrious, determined student.

4. D is a blunt, intelligent, skilful, industrious, determined student.

You may have found that the opposites *warm* and *cold* have a stronger effect on the impressions formed than the traits *polite* or *blunt*. This shows that not all descriptions of traits carry the same weight. Some traits become central, providing the main direction; while others become peripheral and dependent (Ash 1952). (This point is of particular relevance to how we use language in recording observations, to be discussed in Chapter 8.)

First impressions and the dominant impact of certain attributed characteristics may affect the observational process by biasing the observer to seek out information that is consistent with those first impressions and/or the dominant attributed characteristics. Heider (1958) also acknowledges that individuals may ignore or distort evidence which is inconsistent with what they already know or expect. This process is known as *bias towards balance*, where individuals gravitate towards balanced states of mind and away from unbalanced ones in order to maintain mental equilibrium.

Categorisation and stereotyping

When we encounter someone or a social situation for the first time we implicitly organise our first impressions into meaningful categories, based upon prior experience and knowledge. We slot impressions into manageable categories, where pieces of information are loosely held together to provide a sense of order. This categorisation process allows individuals to structure their experience and maintain a sense of order, even though it may be a false one (Calhoun and Acocella 1990; Leyens and Codol 1988).

The categorisation process becomes particularly important when decisions and judgements are made on the basis of known information or selectively perceived information. For example, in Vignette 6.3 Mrs Crisp, knowing that John's father worked in a menswear shop, judged his behaviour in the light of this information. Similarly, having categorised Mrs Crisp as excellent and warm hearted, the observer was surprised by her remark, bringing her/him into an imbalanced state. For child observers this means that what is observed may not necessarily represent intrinsic qualities of the observed child or adult; instead observations may reflect the observer's well-established categories that are used as a point of reference to make judgements about the observed individuals.

While categorisation is a useful devise to make sense of and order new experiences, its major limitation is that it may *underestimate differences within groups* and *overestimate variations between groups* (Eiser 1990; Leyens and Codol 1988; Taylor 1981). To relate this to child study, if you are aware of the typical development of two-year-old children and you are asked to observe a child of this age, you may fail to observe her/his unique characteristics and qualities. Your existing knowledge may become the overarching category, where individual differences are eclipsed. Similarly, individual differences may be overestimated. If you hold the view that there are considerable cultural differences in children's upbringing and their behaviour, your observations may accentuate these differences, if the observed two-year-old child comes from a different culture.

Categorisation may become particularly problematic if a category is well entrenched, leading to stereotypical thinking. This means that, in the name of maintaining consistency and unity of information related to an established category, observers may seek out information that confirms rather than refutes stereotypes (Stangor and Rumble 1989; Stangor 1988). This could be the case, for example, if you are asked to observe a boy who is thought to have symptoms of attention deficit disorder. Having some preconceptions about the symptomatic behaviour of the disorder, as an observer you may attend and record only behaviours that fit into these preconceptions, failing to attend to a wide range and variation of behaviours.

Emotional factors

In order to understand the observation process we also need to consider the role of the observer's emotional state and its impact on potential perceptual and inferential biases. Often observing may become difficult and even painful, because it triggers memories from childhood experiences (positive or negative);

it reawakens current preoccupations and concerns; and it activates a whole tranche of uncomfortable feelings (e.g. being uncertain as an observer or feeling incompetent etc.). These emotional states may colour our perceptions and interpretations of the observations, resulting in attributing characteristics and projecting feelings that may not necessarily belong to the observed child, but to the observer who identifies with her/him.

Psychodynamic theories provide us with a framework, explaining how our own childhood experiences may lead to *defence mechanisms*. Sigmund Freud (1960) postulated a model of unconscious mental processes with three components: *Id, Ego* and *Superego*. The *Id* is full of fears, anxieties and instinctual drives. The *Superego* is the rule maker, acting as an internal, severe parent. The *Ego* is striving to mediate the competing messages from the *Id* and *Superego* in order to provide a state of mental equilibrium.

Unresolved inner conflicts during childhood may lead to a range of defence mechanisms, such as identification, projection, intellectualisation, to maintain mental equilibrium. For example, in Vignette 6.2 the observer identified with Annie to project her own feelings about being too eager to please. Intellectualisation, as a defence mechanism, means that the observer dismisses completely the role of feeling.

For observers, understanding the role of 'defence mechanisms' can provide clues in unpacking what belongs to 'self' (the observer) and what is projected to the 'other' (the observed child). In this model, however, because of the postulated power of the unconscious processes, not everything can be brought to consciousness and explained. Piontelli (1986) has well illustrated the emotional aspect of observation, by acknowledging that sometimes her observations were upsetting and almost unbearable. In effect, when we observe we react and respond to our stimulus 'in thought, feeling and action' (Cook 1979:2).

Recognising bias

It is evident that, although not at the forefront of our minds, attitudes and feelings can exert a strong pressure on what and how we observe. However, these mental processes are not static. As we progress with our observations we may come to form different ideas, to empathise or identify with the observed child, to dislike certain behaviours and actions. We therefore need to recognise, acknowledge, constantly scrutinise and, if necessary, challenge our attitudes to enhance self-awareness.

Consider the list below, and decide whether some characteristics are more appealing or emotive than others, and/or whether they may create certain expectations:

- being a girl or boy;

- a particular name (e.g. Apple, Janet, William, JJ etc.);

- ethnicity or nationality (e.g. French, Albanian, Peruvian, Greek, Italian etc.);

- hair colour (e.g. fair, dark, ginger, brown, dyed etc.);

- behaviour and personality characteristics (e.g. good at learning, confident, alert, warm, boisterous, excitable, helpful, quiet, shy, cheeky, bored, withdrawn etc.);

- appearance (e.g. clean, appropriate clothing, good skin complexion, overweight etc.);

- needing special care, attention and support (e.g. a child with allergies, special needs such as loss of hearing or vision, hyperactivity or attention deficit disorder, Down's syndrome or autism etc.);

- interested parents, non-interfering parents, fussy parents, parent governors, immigrant parents etc.;

- children in care, grieving children, neglected children.

The list above may not allow you to recognise deep-seated prejudices, but identifying your particular preferences may enable you to think about factors that may potentially bias your perceptions of observed children. Open discussions with tutors and peers in reflective sessions (to be discussed in Chapter 9) about your personal and professional likes and dislikes, preferences, priorities and strong feelings will help you to explore potential biases and find their roots. A willingness to analyse how your own beliefs and values are affecting your observations is an important positive characteristic of an observer, sometimes referred to as *personal reflexivity* (Willig 2001). Of course, identifying your unconscious biases is more problematic, but in general, being aware of your attitudes and feelings and relevant processes (see Figure 6.2) is an important step towards counteracting bias.

Figure 6.2 Some of the factors influencing the role of the observer

Summary

Observation as a professional task requires self-awareness and an understanding of the complex, mainly unconscious, mental processes that take place during observation. It is evident that our attitudes determine to a large extent what we see and hear and what we record during observation and how we interpret this. Our tendency to maintain cognitive congruity and consonance may predispose us to seek out information that keeps us in a balanced mental state. Our first impressions of someone or a social situation may filter information that is collected later.

Being consistent with our attitudes and maintaining a balanced state of mind may mean that we build stereotypical categories, where our observed individuals are trapped. The cautionary voice would remind us that our attitudes and expectations should not lead to premature sorting and categorisation of perceived information in order to avoid potential incongruence and dissonance.

Striving for consistency may lead to replication and confirmation of our attitudes and expectations, whereas an open approach to observation may direct us to new, fresh and distinctive understandings. Self-awareness will not be complete without examining our own feelings.

Concluding activity

Revisit Vignettes 6.1 and 6.2 to consider your own interpretation of Annie's observed behaviour.

Chapter 7
Participant and non-participant observation

In this chapter we discuss another aspect of the observer's role, that is, the observer's level of participation and involvement with the activities of the observed child and the setting. We explore the meanings of the terms non-participant and participant observation and consider a continuum of participation. We then discuss observer insider and outsider perspectives and their relevance to the observer's chosen level of participation. Finally, we offer a model of membership that incorporates these ideas.

> ## Vignette 7.1
>
> *Lisa is conducting a non-participant observation of a girl's use of fine motor skills. She seats herself, unobtrusively, in a corner of the classroom where she can see seven-year-old Paige, but she is out of her direct line of vision. At first all goes according to plan and, as Paige completes sentences on a worksheet, Lisa notes Paige's right-handed dynamic tripod grip on the pencil, the way Paige holds the paper still with her left hand, and the fluency and neatness of Paige's letter formation. Then Paige puts down her pencil, momentarily, and the girl next to her takes her pencil and gives her a blunt one in return. Paige objects to this but is told by the teacher to be quiet. Paige then stands up to go to sharpen the blunt pencil and is told by the teaching assistant to sit down. Paige tries to take her own pencil back from the girl but she holds on to it tightly and whispers to Paige that she won't be her friend. Paige puts her head on her hands and is close to tears. The teacher and teaching assistant are engaged in work with other groups of children and are unaware of ther situation.*
>
> *Lisa went over and gave Paige a sharpened pencil. She then returned to her place.*

Introduction

In the vignette above, Lisa conducted a non-participant observation which meant that she both tried to be unobtrusive in the setting and kept her distance from the observed child. However, the situation arose where she felt impelled to participate by intervening to resolve an upsetting incident. We can see that the distinction between a non-participant observer and a participant observer is not always clear cut. The non-participant observer may begin by watching a situation without taking part but might, for practical and ethical reasons, get drawn in and become more actively involved.

In this chapter we begin by discussing non-participant and participant observation and consider a continuum of participation. We then explore the different perspectives, which an observer may take (e.g. insider and outsider) and conclude by discussing observer membership as an alternative model that blends these ideas.

Non-participant observation

Non-participant observation is influenced by scientific traditions of child study that require the observer to record an objective and factual account of the observed child's actions without influencing her/his behaviour in any way. Non-participant observation has the advantage of allowing the observer to focus on the observational task without being distracted by other responsibilities and to keep full and accurate notes. Examples of non-participant observation include the work of Arnold Gesell and Maria Montessori (discussed in Chapter 2). Gesell used especially designed playrooms for the purpose of observing children *unobtrusively*, while Montessori urged observers to *dissociate themselves* from the observed child to maintain scientific objectivity.

In line with these views, some university and research centres have playroom-style laboratories where students can observe young children (e.g. The Tavistock and Portman Clinic). Another way of achieving this is through the use of modern technology such as hidden cameras and pin microphones for covert observations. Gillen and Hall (2001) used this technique to examine children's use of language during their socio-dramatic play in a playhouse in their nursery garden.

As students, it is unlikely that you will be able to conduct covert observations, considering that you need to receive informed consent by those involved (see Chapter 5). Therefore as a non-participant observer you take a *fly-on-the-wall* approach, by being unobtrusive and dissociated from the happenings, and attempting not to influence the situation at all. Perhaps it is easier to be an unobtrusive, non-participant observer in a classroom, where there are many members of staff and children may be used to the arrival of new members of staff and/or visitors. In a home setting such a situation is rather unnatural and awkward and, despite your intention of being unobtrusive, you may have exactly the opposite effect. The child being observed may be intrigued by your presence and behaviour. They may approach and attempt to find out why you are there, what you are doing and why. They may want to involve you in their play or they may wish to be involved with your work. But, once you have become friendly with the children and spent time playing with them it is not easy to retreat into a passive, non-participant role. Therefore it is important to think about where you choose to observe.

Participant observation

Participant observation is a method that comes from research traditions in anthropology and ethnography (Denzin and Lincoln 2000; Hastrup 1995; Spradley 1980) (see Theory box 7.1). It emphasises the subjective nature of the observational process, seeking out the meaning of the experience from within and potentially from the many different perspectives of those being observed

(Bruyn 1966). The observers may already be part of the setting (e.g. practitioners, teachers, parents) in which the observation takes place, being closely involved with children's lives and the daily practice of the setting; or they may join the group under study to become familiar with the people and immerse themselves in their day-to-day activities.

Theory box 7.1

Origins of participant observation

Participant observation has its origins in anthropological research in the late nineteenth and early twentieth centuries. Anthropologists, such as Frank Hamilton Cushing, Bronislaw Malinowski, Edward Evans-Pritchard and Margaret Mead, travelled to various parts of the world to study, record and analyse different ways of life. In order to gain insights into the cultures of these non-Western societies they befriended their informants, became integrated into local communities and took part in their daily activities.

Ethnographic research developed from this type of anthropological cross-cultural study. From the 1920s and 1930s, community studies were carried out by researchers based at the University of Chicago. The works from this 'Chicago School', which focused on studying people in their natural environments, established the importance of capturing, describing and studying human group life in order to represent people's stories and understand social problems. Qualitative researchers, in many academic disciplines, continue to use participant observation as a means of observing and interacting with people in everyday social contexts and as a way of gaining insights through personal experience.

Denzin and Lincoln (2000); Hastrup (1995)

Participant observation has been used in educational settings to provide insights about educational practice from within. For example, Vivian Gussin Paley (1981; 1986; 1988; 1990) has provided thought-provoking case studies of events that took place in the classrooms where she worked as a teacher. Her participant observations provide evidence on which she bases her developing understanding of educational issues such as gender, social development and inclusion. The Danish researcher, Hanne Warming (2005), also used participant observation to appreciate the viewpoints of young children attending an early childhood institution. Taking the *least adult role* (after Corsaro 1985) and doing research *with* the children (after Mayall 2000), she played alongside the children, getting as close to them as possible. She accepted the authority of the adults in charge, taking no responsibility for educating, disciplining or caring for the children. Such total participation as an adult observer is unusual, and students are unlikely to adopt this method. A more usual participant observation stance is one in which the observer engages with the children, while maintaining sufficient separation to be able to observe and take notes.

Observer effect

Even when the observer chooses to be a non-participant, s/he will always be a participant to some extent. By just being in a setting the observer is not only influenced, but s/he also influences and has an effect on those being observed. A similar effect is evident when, for example, the cheering crowds at sports events create an exciting atmosphere and their support motivates the players. A famous example of the effect of the observer on observed people comes from Elton Mayo's study at the Hawthorne Works in Chicago, USA (Roethlisberger and Dickson 1939). This study showed that the mere presence of the observer had a direct impact on the observed workers' productivity. Named after the place where Mayo's studies were conducted the phenomenon of observer effect is also known as the *Hawthorne Effect* (see Theory box 7.2).

Theory box 7.2

The Hawthorne effect

The term *Hawthorne Effect* was coined, with the term *Observer Effect*, as a result of a series of studies carried out in the 1920s, by the National Academy of Sciences with the Western Electric Company at the Hawthorne Works in Chicago, USA. These studies aimed to establish the relationship between different working conditions and workers' productivity. The initial hypothesis was that the workers' productivity would rise as the level of lighting improved and vice versa. The findings of these studies showed that the level of productivity was not directly connected to the lighting level. One of the hypotheses was that increased productivity was due to the workers' awareness of being observed. This hypothesis was tested, and confirmed that levels of productivity were stimulated by the attention of the observers rather than the lighting level.

Roethlisberger and Dickson (1939)

A *fly on the wall* presence may minimise the observer effect, especially if you are in a busy classroom that makes it easy for you to blend into the daily activity without attracting the children's attention. In line with ethical practice, however, you would expect the teacher, or the person in charge, to introduce you to the children, explaining who you are and what you are doing there. Inevitably this introduction draws the children's attention to you and may lead to observer effect, in that the children present their 'best' selves or demonstrate behaviours they assume you want to observe. As a result, you observe behaviours that are not necessarily typical of those that take place when you are not present.

The question then is how do you observe the actual behaviours of your observed children rather than their acts? What will you do? A strategy may be that you take some time before the observations to visit the setting and become familiar to those whom you intend to observe. This has benefits because everybody gets used to the observer, relaxes, and their behaviours are likely to be more typical. This strategy can impact on the observer's position as non-participant, because the insights gained may alter the observation process and recordings. The observer's closeness to the setting and emotional response to the happenings or individual children's circumstances may decrease her/his distance, leading to observer bias (discussed in Chapter 6).

Clearly, both observer effect and observer bias are present in all observations, but the degree of their impact on the observation process depends on the length of time spent in a setting and the observer's level of participation. Usually the observer effect is stronger when the non-participant observer enters the setting for the first time. As the novelty of the observer presence wears off and the observer becomes part of the setting her/his impact on the observed individuals becomes weaker. This is especially true with children, although the observer effect may have a longer and stronger impact on adults.

The discussion of observer effect highlights the complexity of observation, which is not merely an act of recording the behaviour of another person. It is a process of interactions between the observer and the observed, who influence and are influenced by each other (to be discussed further in Chapter 8). It is important for the observer, as shown in the vignette above, to be attuned to the changes occurring throughout the observation process and how this might affect what is attended to and recorded.

A continuum of observer participation

In the descriptions of non-participant and participant observation, there are some distinctive features (see Table 7.1). In reality, the boundaries between non-participation and participation are often blurred. Looking at Vignette 7.1, would you describe the observer as being non-participant or participant? It is evident that, while the observer entered the observation as non-participant, she felt that circumstances drew her into a participant response.

Rather than viewing non-participant and participant observation as distinct opposites, it is possible to view them on a continuum of observer participation (Adler and Adler 1987; Gold 1958). The observer continuum implies that the observer may drift and shift at any points between the two extremes (Figure 7.1).

As a student it is likely that you would take the role of non-participant observer, but circumstances, as shown in Vignette 7.1, may lead you to become an *observer-as-participant*. As a practitioner, who might also be a student conducting an observation within the workplace, you start from *complete participation*, but your observations may require that you move on to *participant-as-observer*. Theoretically, as Figure 7.1 shows, an observer can shift from one extreme of participation to the other in either direction. The question posed here is whether someone who is a complete participant can ever become a complete non-participant observer. The answer lies in how we understand participation.

Table 7.1 Key characteristics of non-participant and participant observation

Non-participant observation	Participant observation
The observer maintains her/his distance, is neutral, sees from 'without'	The observer is immersed in the situation, sees from 'within'
Focus on scientific/objective recordings and understandings	Focus on subjective understandings and meanings
Conducted in both laboratory and naturalistic settings	Conducted in naturalistic settings

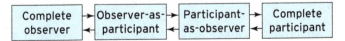

Figure 7.1 The continuum of observer participation (after Gold 1958)

At a basic level, participation may be understood in terms of the observer's location in the setting and level of physical involvement with the children's activities. At another level, participation may take the form of emotional and psychological involvement rather than active engagement with daily routine and activities. Observers bring to the observation their own attitudes and experiences, emotions, and prior knowledge that might unintentionally create a commitment to engage with the observed child (as discussed in Chapter 6). In addition, as the observation progresses, the observer accrues more insider knowledge about the observed child that cannot be ignored. You cannot undo what you already know and, as a result, this knowledge may influence your stance as an observer. The emotional and psychological processes and accrued insider knowledge are less obvious and visible dimensions of participation. Nonetheless in an unconscious manner they influence the observer's shift across the continuum of participation.

To return to the question whether a complete participant can become a complete non-participant observer, we need to consider the multifaceted and complex nature of participation. You might decide to distance yourself physically from the observed child and attempt to dissociate yourself from what you know, but as a complete participant you have gained insider perspectives that become part of your pre-existing knowledge which compromise your position as a non-participant. Thus, it is unlikely a complete participant can become a non-participant observer.

Insider and outsider perspectives

Insider and outsider perspectives are two other concepts associated with observation. These concepts are also known as *emic*-insider and *etic*-outsider perspectives in ethnographic research (see Fetterman 1998). Insider observers study a group to which they belong, while outsider observers are strangers to the group they observe. For example, if you are observing a child in your workplace, then you might be described as being an *insider*, whereas if you are a student who visits a nursery class for the first time, you would be described as an *outsider*.

An *insider* perspective is usually achieved by an observer who actively joins the activities of a child or setting. The aim of insider observers is to enter as fully as possible into the life of children they study and to gain a deep insight, through seeing the world in similar ways. This perspective requires detailed observations that allow somebody else, who reads them, to appreciate children's experiences, as in the work of Warming (2005).

The insider observer has the advantage of a broad and deep knowledge of the context of her/his observations and the child's behaviour within this context. A disadvantage of this position is that the insider may miss something obvious just because it is so familiar. In addition, there is a danger that the insider may be so influenced by the surrounding culture that it is difficult to be impartial and to make balanced judgements about the situation. Greater familiarity can lead to a loss of objectivity particularly in terms of unintentionally making erroneous assumptions or biased interpretations (Breen 2007).

In contrast, an *outsider* perspective is taken by observers who are not familiar with the children or the setting. They observe and try to provide an objective account of what is happening. For instance, if you are new to the nursery where you will carry out your observations and have not worked with young children before you will approach the situation as an outsider with a fresh viewpoint. However, an outsider's presence may become obtrusive and interfere with the normal daily activity (observer effect). For this reason, the role of the outsider observer is more likely to work better in large nursery classes, playgrounds or public spaces rather than in confined spaces such as a family setting (Jorgensen 1989).

Outsider observers understand observations in scientific terms. They aim to maintain objectivity by attempting to capture information and impressions that may not be noticed by insiders. They are likely to use methods of observation that yield quantitative and/or comparable data (e.g checklists, rating scale). Observations collected from an outsider perspective may claim to be more objective than the observations recorded by an insider. The disadvantages of this position are the observer effect and the lack of an understanding of the context for their observations.

As an observer, it may be possible to hold both insider and outsider perspectives, although to a different degree, as the following examples demonstrate. Consider, for example, the following:

- You are an overseas student who has never visited the UK before and never studied early childhood; you are likely to be a complete outsider when you visit a nursery school in the UK for the first time.

- You are a parent who, as a student, is required to conduct a child study in an early years setting; here you might have insider perspectives of children's development as a parent, but hold an outsider perspective of early years practice.

- You are an experienced practitioner, who has general insider perspectives of early years practice, but when you visit a new early years setting for the first time (e.g. overseas), you hold an outsider's perspective of the practice of this setting.

Clearly, as is the case with participation, we can think of insider/outsider perspectives on a continuum.

Knott (2005) states that the insider/outsider perspectives correspond with participant/non-participant observations, respectively. However, it is possible to conceptualise insider/outsider perspectives and participant/non-participant observations in different ways. An observer can be either an insider or outsider and choose to conduct either a participant or non-participant observation. This relationship is represented in Figure 7.2, where the insider/outsider and participant/non-participant perspectives are seen as intersecting continua. In this diagram the two dimensions are differentiated, allowing the observer to position her/himself anywhere on the two continua. The choice made determines the method of observation and affects the recording, the data collected and the understandings gained.

Taking an outsider and non-participant stance increases objectivity, but it decontextualises the understandings of the observed child. Being an outsider aiming to conduct participant observations may enhance the observer's understanding

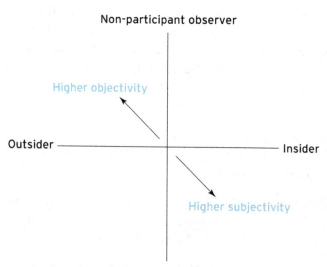

Figure 7.2 The intersecting continua of insider-outsider perspectives and participant/non-participant observation, influencing the degree of subjectivity-objectivity

of the experience of the observed child within context, but it becomes less objective. Being an insider and conducting a non-participant observation ignores contextual understandings by aiming to increase objectivity. Finally, being an insider and conducting participant observations gives complete subjective understandings of the experiences of those being observed, but objectivity diminishes. In general, it is assumed that an outsider/non-participant perspective produces more objective observations, whereas insider/participant provides more subjective ones.

The diagrammatic representation in Figure 7.2 attempts to simplify a complex, illusive and ambiguous observer role, witnessed even in the works of great scholars such as Darwin and Isaacs (see Vignettes 2.1 and 2.2). As an observer then you need to be mindful of what you bring into the observation process and what you want to find out to clarify your position and explore the range of dilemmas posed at a practical level. For example, as an outsider, who wants to conduct a participant observation, you will need to gain insider perspectives by being actively involved with the activities of the child or the setting. This however may not be feasible or acceptable.

From the discussion above, you may start thinking that the positioning as non-participant observer taking an outsider perspective is unlikely. This is because (i) we all carry existing knowledge, expectations and assumptions that we bring into observations, (ii) our mere presence changes the setting as we enter it and (iii) our accrued knowledge from observations over time negates the detached view. Starting from this point of view, Adler and Adler (cited in Angrosino and Mays de Pérez 2003) propose an alternative framework of observer membership within the observed setting. They suggest three levels of membership, that is: *complete member*, totally immersed and affiliated; *active member*, affiliated but not committed to all the values; and *peripheral member*, developing desirable insider perspectives, without participation in the activities.

Summary

In this chapter we discussed non-participant and participant observation, insider and outsider perspectives and the observer effect. We have suggested that it is more helpful to view the two dimensions of participant/non-participant and insider/outsider as two intersecting continua rather than as two distinct dimensions. The positioning across those two continua will influence the type of observations undertaken and the recordings made. Observer membership is another way of thinking about the level of observer involvement.

Concluding activity

Consider the aims of your observation and write down in your Learning Diary where you intend to position yourself across the continua of participant/non-participant and insider-outsider perspectives. You should reflect on subsequent observations to see how this positioning might have changed over time.

Part II
Conducting and interpreting child observation

Chapter 8
Conducting and recording narrative observations

In this chapter we discuss issues that relate to the actual processes of conducting and recording observations. We first explore some of the challenges experienced by observers during observations. We look at the requirements for producing informative observational records and conclude by seeing observation as a context of dynamic interactions between the observed, the observer and the observation context.

Vignette 8.1

Alki, a four year old, joined the nursery school in April and attends the morning sessions three days a week. Alki has been described by her mother and staff as having 'separation anxiety'. Two students who have been visiting the nursery school were asked to observe and record Alki's behaviour throughout the morning session, as non-participant observers. Informed written consent was received from staff and Alki's mother as well as Alki herself. Below are two short excerpts from both observational records.

Excerpt from observational record 1

Alki sits on the carpet with one arm leaning on her teacher. Another girl is sat opposite, with a book in between them. The teacher reads a page of the book and then asks the girls what the pictures are and to count them. There are two butterflies on the page. Alki tells the teacher about a time she touched a butterfly.

Teacher:	*'Did the butterfly look like the one in the picture?'*
Alki:	*'No. It looked different'.*
Teacher:	*'You must be careful with butterflies . . .'*

The teacher carries on reading the book and asking questions. The other girl sitting with them answers most of the questions. Alki is still leaning on her teacher. She looks up at her teacher, when she makes the noises of animals.

When the last page of the story is opened, Alki kneels up and stands, walks outside and checks the weather. She says: 'It's not raining, so we can go out.'

The teacher gets her raincoat and she goes to the door.

Alki:	*'Wait for me.' She runs to her peg and grabs her coat. She puts it on herself. The teacher walks outside holding hands with Alki.*

Excerpt from observational record 2

Alki is sitting on the carpet area, clinging on to her teacher. Another girl is sitting opposite them. The teacher reads a book about animals. Before she turns over the page, she asks the girls some questions. (I can't hear the questions nor the girls' answer; I am sitting quite far away, so as not to be noticed by Alki.)

From time to time, Alki looks at me; I smile and turn my attention quickly to my notepad. She looks away shyly! She then gets up hurriedly and walks out of the classroom; she runs back and says in an excited voice: 'It is not raining; can we go out?'

The teacher and the two girls put their coats on and walk out of the class. Being conscious that Alki was aware of my presence, I waited for a while before I followed them outside.

Introduction

The vignette above shows us that conducting observations is not always a straightforward task. The two observers looked at the same child, in the same context and at the same time, yet the observation records differ in terms of their length, detail, and the kind of information they contain. The first observer provided a detailed observational record that describes the observed event and participants' interactions. The second observer produced a shorter observation record that lacks detail and, in some instances, the language is inferential rather than descriptive. Clearly, s/he is conscious of the observer role.

Even in systematic observations it is not possible to have a consensus on what has been observed and recorded. Differences may be partly explained in terms of the perceptual process, where our own attitudes, past knowledge and experience, and expectations for the future influence our perceptions of the observed child within the context (as discussed in Chapter 6). However, the actual process of doing observations presents its own challenges. Observers, and especially novice observers, often raise questions and concerns such as:

- Where should I position myself and what distance should I keep from the observed child or situation?

- What should I do as a non-participant observer, if the child or the adult in charge interacts with me or needs my attention?

- What should I do if I feel uncomfortable with the demands of the adult in charge or the educational and care practices?

These types of questions closely relate to the role of the observer, such as whether s/he is a non-participant, participant or s/he shifts and changes role (Creswell 2007).

Observer's position

Non-participant observers often face the dilemma of where to position them-selves in the educational setting or family context, if applicable, and the dis-tance they should maintain from the observed child. If the observer sits too far away from the observed child then it is likely that information, especially lan-guage and conversation details, will be missed, as was the case with the second observer in Vignette 8.1. Yet, if sitting too close it is likely that the observer will attract the child's immediate attention and this may result in observer effect. Another dilemma is whether to follow the observed child if s/he moves out of sight. Not to follow the child means that the observer misses out on aspects of her/his behaviour. To follow the child may mean that s/he is reminded of the observer's presence, triggering or reinforcing the observer effect. In addition and more importantly, some children may become self-conscious, feel obliged to conform and perform or feel uncomfortable and even withdrawn because of the observer's overt presence.

General advice is that observers should maintain some distance from the observed child and act like *a fly on the wall* to minimise the observer effect. But, however subtly the observer positions her/himself, it is likely that s/he will be noticed. Having asked for the child's informed assent (see Chapter 5) it is almost certain that s/he will be aware of the observer's presence, although over time the child may forget or ignore the fact that they are being watched.

We therefore suggest that any decision you take is informed by, and bal-ances, two basic considerations. First, the child's safety and well-being is your main priority at all times, in any situation and for any purpose (BERA 2004). Second, your chosen location and position should be unobtrusive and not interfere with the everyday functioning of the setting or the child's activities, while offering you adequate visibility to access and record what is happen-ing (Sternberg 2005; Delamont 2002). Any sign of distress on the child's part means the observation should be interrupted, independently of how important you may consider your observational data to be. Ultimately there is no simple or universal answer to the dilemmas faced by observers and, for any decision you take you should carefully weigh its advantages and disadvantages against the fundamental principle of the welfare of the child and record the reasons for your decisions in your Learning Diary.

Responding to children and situations

Another dilemma often faced by observers is whether to respond to children's interactions and other events. Interacting with the child may shift the observer's chosen stance (e.g. becoming a fuller participant), but by not responding the observer may feel irresponsible or at odds with the situation. This is illustrated in the example below, where a student was conducting a non-participant observation at the family home, observing a three-and-a-half-year-old-child.

The little boy took me to see a map of the world on his bedroom wall. He pointed to a dot and wondered what it was – I suggested a tiny island. I struggled hard to identify the observer role, especially with a child for whom pro-social interactions were so important.

On another occasion the observer consciously decided to step outside the non-participant observer role, in order to prevent a potential accident. The observer recorded:

When I was in the garden with the twins, while the mother was attending to one twin, the other child got into a dangerous position on the climbing frame, so I had to intervene to prevent her from hurting herself.

Evidently, while you will carefully prepare for your work, observation can sometimes catch you unawares and you have to respond quickly. You will need to make quick judgements about a situation, react to children's interactions and actions, and make decisions that safeguard the child's well-being and safety. You may record your responses to these situations and their impact on the observational record in your Learning Diary. If relevant, you may also reflect about the appropriateness of conducting non-participant observations in family settings.

Contextual challenges

Observations and observational records are also subject to contextual factors and events. Even when the observer has reached an understanding with the adults in charge (e.g. parents or early years professionals) and has negotiated and established a place, sometimes there is a need to explain and reiterate the observer role. For example, an observer recorded in her Learning Diary:

I was left in the home doing a child observation while the mother 'popped to the shops'. So I had to explain that I was not there to be responsible for the child. This was difficult because I felt I owed something to the family that allowed me to observe at their home.

Another observer noted:

I felt that the mother wanted my attention to the exclusion of the child. I resolved this situation by delicately negotiating with the mother to spend separate time with her before starting to observe both of them together.

Similarly, an observer recorded:

Ali's learning support assistant constantly pointed out to me behaviours which I should notice and record, e.g. how neatly Ali was writing; how well he was playing with other children. She wanted to know what I was thinking about Ali's achievements and progress and about her support for him. I felt I had no expertise to make any judgements, but I was concerned that I may disappoint her; she seemed to work so hard and conscientiously with Ali.

These reflections show that observers often change their role and stances because of circumstances beyond their control. The examples demonstrate that contextual factors may create additional dilemmas and pressure on observers, requiring delicate renegotiation, or may leave them ambivalent and uncertain how to deal with the situation.

How these challenges are addressed depends on your own skills and confidence to reiterate the purpose of your observations and renegotiate your role with the adult in charge, but the existing or developing relationship with your hosts may need to be examined. Conducting your observation in a friend's home may make it difficult to draw the boundaries between informal friendly rela-tionships and the professional stance required for your observation. Similarly, doing observations in an educational setting, where staff have been helpful and accommodating, you may feel obliged to follow their suggestions and compro-mise the initial purpose of your observation.

There is no single answer to these or similar dilemmas, but you are more likely to avoid awkward situations if you approach observations in a professional manner. Following on from your participant information letter (discussed in Chapter 5), you may take the opportunity during your first visit to reiterate the purpose of your observation and clarify your expectations and those of your host. If you feel that the relationship with your host is such that professional boundaries cannot be main-tained, it could be better to consider a different setting for your observations.

If, as a student, in a professional context you feel unsure about how to deal with a situation, you should discuss your dilemmas with your tutor and perhaps with your fellow students in reflective seminars (to be discussed in Chapter 9) to gain clarity and receive practical suggestions. As a general rule, independently of where you conduct your observations, it is important that you approach them as a professional task, guided by the principle that the children's interests and well-being are of paramount importance. As the research ethics committees of universities and colleges increasingly assume responsibility for students' field-work activities related to their learning (discussed in Chapter 5), they expect students to conduct their observations in a professional manner.

Conducting observations as part of everyday regular duties and responsibilities as a practitioner may eliminate some of these challenges, but creates others. For example, how much time could you give to your observation, while deal-ing with everyday life in your setting? Would other duties and responsibilities distract you from your observations? How could you systematically record the observed behaviours and actions, while at the same time you interact with the child and other children?

Recording narrative observations

Observers are also confronted with challenges related to the recording of observations. Student observers in particular, when they start doing observa-tions, often ask questions such as: What and when should I record? Do I write up my observations as I observe or do I do this after the observational session? Should I use different media to record my observations, such as photos, tape- or video-recordings? What kind of information should I include and how much detail do I need in my observational records? How do I record non-verbal com-munication, responses and acts?

Noticing and note taking

Our challenge as observers is to capture as much relevant data as possible dur-ing the time spent observing. Most observers take notes at the time of observa-tion, but find it impossible to maintain a full account of all information; critical moments and incidents may be missed while concentrating on note taking. If they rely on memory alone to record an observation, they may realise that memory fades quickly or rearranges the order of events to preserve consist-ency and cognitive congruity (as discussed in Chapter 6).

One way to increase the accuracy and detail of observational records is the use of aide-memoires that will trigger your memory when you write up your observations. Some of the aide-memoires you can employ include: note taking in a chronological order and at regular intervals; noting specific incidents and key events; mapping and tracking the child's movement diagrammatically. All of these are specific methods of recording observations (discussed in Chapter 3), but you can also use them as aide-memoires for narrative records. Noting down key words and phrases, drawing diagrams or sketches, or using shorthand abbreviations should enable you to recall the events later and elicit details to produce a fuller observation record (Delamont 2002). You may include your aide-memoires in your Learning Diary.

Photographs, audio- or video-recordings may be used as tools for obtaining a fuller record, but you will need to consider ethical issues of parental, child and staff consent, and secure management of data (see Chapter 5). These methods can be intrusive and, before negotiating their use, you should consider their appropriateness for the kind of observation you wish to conduct. The advantages of these methods, for instance achieving an accurate permanent record of a child's spoken language, have to be balanced against the disadvantages of increased observer effect. For example, the child may be reluctant to speak if aware of the recording and the surrounding adults become self-conscious. Even if you choose to make an audio- or video-recording, the observation will still be partial as you have to select what to focus on and which perspective to take, so other potential data will be missed.

By being systematic and methodical in developing and using aide-memoires and recording strategies you will be able to capture a wealth of data that is of interest, preserves detail and increases explicitness (Delamont 2002; Weick 1985). It is important, however, that any observation notes are revisited and used very soon after the completion of the observation, when memories are at the front of the mind, in order to write the full observational record.

The power of language

In non-participant narrative observations, such as those in Vignette 8.1, observers are advised to record, in a detached and objective manner, all sensory data (i.e. what is seen, heard, smelt, felt), avoiding inferential or judgemental language. Observational records are expected to be descriptive, using a neutral language that avoids instantaneous or premature judgements. For example, the writer of the second observation excerpt may be criticised for saying 'clinging on to her teacher' and 'she looks away shyly'; as these involve judgement about the child's behaviours. The author in the first observational excerpt, in contrast, records: 'Alki sits on the carpet with one arm leaning on her teacher'. This description of the child's positioning in relation to the teacher is open to interpretation by readers. In reality, observation involves a dual perceptual and inferential process that is difficult to separate during the observations, but can be addressed when narrative observation records are written up, and during reflections.

Another issue relates to the kind of detail included in the observational record. Should an observer include the statement 'It was a very grey day when I went into the classroom with the bright yellow door'? The answer is not straightforward. If this is a description that is not relevant to the aims of the observation, then it may be left out. For example, it is unlikely to have a place in an observation of an individual child's motor skills, but it could be relevant to an observation about the learning environment. Additionally, if this description is indicative of the observer's feelings and mood, which may have impacted on the observation process, then this statement may be noted in the observer's Learning Diary. Ultimately, what is included in the observational record is determined by the purpose and type of the observation conducted.

The use of language plays an important role in producing observational records that portray to a reader an accurate picture of the observed child, situation or event. As an observer you need to be constantly aware of, and alert to, the use of language, especially in describing non-verbal communication such as gestures, body movements and positioning, physiological reactions, different emotions, moods and affects (Cohen et al. 1997). Compare the use of language by the two observers in Vignette 8.1. The first observer provides a picture of Alki's moves when she writes '[she] kneels up and stands, walks outside', allowing the reader to visualise the movements of the child, whereas the second observer briefly noted the action by stating 'She . . . gets up hurriedly', offering less description and more judgement.

Observation – a context of dynamic interactions

Some individuals may be temperamentally more suited to systematic observation than others, but anybody can be trained to become a methodical observer. In practical terms, this means that as an observer:

- you are prepared to deal with unexpected challenges;
- you are able to develop self-awareness and examine your own values and biases;

- you are prepared to experiment with aide-memoires to enable the recall of information;

- you notice and record non-verbal cues such as gestures, physiological and motor responses and reactions;

- you use appropriate language and tone to produce detailed and accurate observational records.

Although there is general advice about conducting and recording sound observations, ultimately decisions will be specific to the purpose of your observation, guided by your priority to safeguard children's well-being and to respect the setting where the observations take place.

Observation is *a context of dynamic interactions*, where *the observer*, *the observed* and *the context* are continuously and dynamically defined and redefined, positioned and repositioned, and influence and are influenced by each other (Angrosino and Mays de Pérez 2003) (Figure 8.1). This means that factors relating to each interacting entity (the observer, the observed and the context) may potentially obstruct or distract and even block the focus of the observation (explored further in Chapter 15).

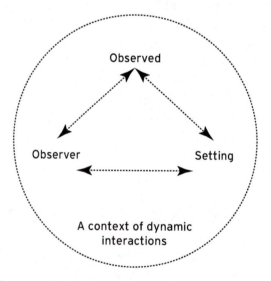

Figure 8.1 Observation – a context of dynamic interactions

Summary

In this chapter we discussed issues which observers often experience when conducting and recording observations in a professional manner. These include observer positioning, responding to children or others in the setting, noticing and note taking, and the use of language in recording. In the light of these issues, we see observation as *a context of dynamic interactions*, between the observer, the observed and the setting.

Concluding activity

Knowing the setting where your observation will be conducted, think about the aide-memoires that would be most appropriate to use in order to write up your narrative observation record.

Chapter 9
Observation and the reflective process

In this chapter we discuss the reflective process in observation. We start by exploring the concept of reflection and continue by discussing reflection *in action* and reflection *on action* and the affective processes involved. We conclude with a discussion of reflective dialogues and four lenses of reflection.

Vignette 9.1

Observation record (Description of sensory information)	Reflections on observation (Observer's thoughts and feelings)
Adam (aged 22 months), who has just woken up, runs over to the slide in his back garden making babbling noises. As he approaches the slide Adam grips on to the ladder with both hands and lifts his legs up off the ground. Adam then pulls himself up the ladder to the top of the slide, assisted by his mother. She then picks Adam up, as he approaches the top of the slide, and helps him to sit down. Adam starts to scream loudly. His mother holds on to him while he slides down the slide. Adam laughs and babbles as he slides down and approaches the bottom of the slide.	Full of energy after his sleep Gaining strength in arms and legs – can coordinate climbing slide steps Is this the best way of supporting him? Does he scream because he doesn't like being at this height or because he wants to do this independently? Mood changes quickly back to a positive one

Introduction

Being thoughtful is important at all stages of the observation process. The notes alongside the observation record in Vignette 9.1 capture the observer's thoughts during the observation and initial reflections as s/he was writing the observation record. These reflective notes and observation record form the basis for further thinking and reflection.

In this chapter we consider the meaning and processes of reflection. We discuss reflection *in action* and reflection *on action* and its affective dimension. Reflective dialogues and different lenses of reflection are also considered. Together these steps are important for interrogating personal attitudes and values before embarking on the systematic analysis of observations.

What is reflection?

John Dewey (1991:6) defined reflection as 'active, persistent, and careful consideration of any belief or supposed form of knowledge in the light of the grounds that support it and the further conclusions to which it tends'. This dynamic process of thinking also applies to observational experiences that, when examined in relation to what is already known, can help observers to make sense of them and apply new insights. Students on childhood courses are often required to use reflection as part of their learning and many teachers, nurses, social workers and counsellors engage in reflection in their professional work. This can be carried out alone or with others, as discussed later in this chapter.

Reflecting on what you observe is important in making sense of the observations and beginning to form new ideas and knowledge. Rather than simply accepting what you observed at face value, reflection means looking in more depth at your observation records, questioning, and seeing different possibilities, in order to understand what you have observed more thoroughly. Several theories of education incorporate this reflective aspect of the learning process, and there are various theoretical models of reflection and reflective practice. Here we will refer back to some of the educational theories mentioned in Chapter 1 and also introduce ideas from well-known reflective models (e.g. Brookfield 1995; Gibbs 1988; Schön 1983) and consider their relevance to the observational process.

Piaget (2001) explained how understanding is gained by the process of linking new information with what is already known (assimilation within an existing schema) or by adjusting and restructuring ideas to think about something differently (accommodation involving the creation of a new schema). Dewey (1991), writing as an educational philosopher rather than as a psychologist, described a similar process of making sense of situations and gaining new insights through a process of linking what is observed with what we already know. Piaget's and Dewey's theories, of connecting what one sees with what one knows and can discover more about, have been described as learning through experience. In the case of the vignette above, the observer's reflective notes reveal that she is making sense of what she sees, for example linking the child's energy levels with being refreshed from having had a sleep and making judgements about his motor skills. She also expresses questions that reveal the possibility of learning something new about the child, understanding his emotional expression and considering the best ways of supporting his development of certain skills.

Reflection *in action* and reflection *on action*

Schön (1983) writes of the significance of both reflection in action, having an awareness of what you are doing while you are involved in an activity, and reflection on action, looking back on an experience to gain deeper insights. An observer's initial reflective comments show reflection in action, while jotting down what came to mind when watching the child. These are more likely to be initial responses and reactions, in thought and feeling, that need to be separated from the sensory information as we suggested in Chapter 3 (see Figure 3.2). This written record then offers a tool for reflection on action, looking back at what was seen and thinking about it. The reflection on action can occur while typing up the observation, reflecting with peers and tutors, reviewing relevant reading, and in preparation for the analysis of your observations. Reading the reflections of someone else's observation (as in Vignette 9.1, right-hand column) it is not clear which reflections occurred *in action* or which were added when reflecting *on action*. For your own observations you will be aware of a distinction between the thoughts you had at the time of observing and the notes you added afterwards. Together these form your reflections on observation that will form part of your overall Learning Diary.

Affective aspects of reflection

Gibbs (1988) describes an expanded model of reflection that includes awareness of feelings. This approach to reflection allows you to take feelings into account when thinking about the meanings of what you have observed (see Figure 9.1). Considering any emotions that the observation evoked can contribute to the process of interpretation, that is, making sense of what has been observed and possibly learning something meaningful from it.

For example, in relation to Vignette 9.1, the observer's questioning feelings about the mother's support may add to an understanding of appropriate ways to facilitate children's motor skills. Was this the most effective way to scaffold Adam's attempts to use the slide and manage the tricky transition between climbing up the ladder and then getting into a sitting position to go down the slide? You might react differently, depending upon whether you are keen to foster a child's independence or are eager to uphold high standards of supervision and safety. It is because people have different ideas and perspectives on children's care and learning that it is useful to reflect on observations with others, as well as independently.

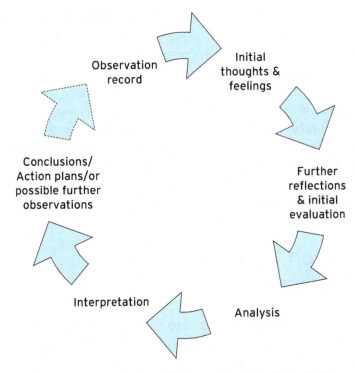

Figure 9.1 A reflective process applied to child observation (after Gibbs 1988)

Reflective dialogue

Personal reflection can be a way of learning from observations, but it is often difficult to question your own assumptions and see alternative ways of interpreting what you saw. Discussing and reflecting upon your observations with others can provide additional insights and understandings. Peer group discussions facilitated by tutors may extend the reflective process. Based on the rationale that learning is socially constructed, reflection with peers can be important for creating and sharing learning. Peers can help the observer to question her/his assumptions, recognise bias, and check out details and accuracy of observations. Peers can relate to observations shared with them, ask revealing questions and provide potential alternative insights. The role of the tutor is to facilitate shared reflections and scaffold students' learning by introducing concepts and ideas from relevant theories to inform and enrich what has been observed. Shared reflections also function as supportive forums for observers to discuss specific issues and challenges that they experience. However, observers should be mindful of the fact that shared reflections may evoke strong feelings in other participants, necessitating sensitive handling.

The shared reflections may be tutor led or you may set up your own peer group. Whichever is the case, the group will have to set ground rules that take into account ethical principles. These rules may include preserving the anonymity of children, families and settings, and maintaining confidentiality by not discussing what is spoken about outside the group. There may also be agreements about what participants will prepare and bring to the group, for example each week a different person may come prepared with copies of her/his observation and be ready to lead a discussion about it. Whatever ground rules are agreed upon, the most important characteristic of the group should be mutual respect. This will include both respect within the group, appreciating one another's work and opinions, and a respectful attitude towards the observed child and his or her setting.

Reflecting on the quality of observation records

Reflection on observation can be used to evaluate the quality of the observational record. The observer should consider whether the observation record is accurate and detailed enough to give all the information needed to address the aims of the observation. For example, Vignette 9.1 was carried out in order to study Adam's gross motor skills. Does the observation give the reader detailed information about his movements? Could the phrase 'runs over to the slide' be written more descriptively to allow the reader to envisage his running action and make judgements about his motor abilities? For a more detailed and sophisticated analysis of motor ability, which takes into account the individual, her/his action and the environment (Thelen and Smith 1996), information could be included about the surface on which the child was running (e.g. long grass, short grass, smooth paving stones, or gravel) as well as exactly how he performed the running movement. It will not be possible to add to the current observation record, as extra information from memory could be inaccurate. However, being reflectively self-critical will enable you to prepare a more detailed account in the future. The quality of the observation record is important, as the analysis and interpretation relies on accuracy and detail of the original records.

Four lenses of reflection

Stephen Brookfield (1995), writing about reflection on the process of teaching adults, proposes four lenses of reflection: the self, students' perspectives, colleagues' views and theoretical literature. These lenses can also provide a useful basis for reflection about child observation: first, reflecting on your own (self); second, reflecting with peers (student perspective); third, reflecting with practitioners and, when appropriate, with parents; and fourth, reflecting in the light of theories that could apply. The four lenses of reflection are discussed in turn.

Reflecting on your own

The lens of *self* starts when you first write up the observation record and separate sensory information from your thoughts and feelings. It continues with reflection on action. For example, you might think about situations in your own life that may affect how you think about what you have seen. Taking Vignette 9.1 as an example, if you have happy memories of playing on a slide when young you might perceive the activity positively and see that the child enjoyed it; whereas if you were intimidated by playground equipment or experienced an accident you could fear for the child's safety. The observation record in Vignette 9.1 is a document for sharing and discussion, so that other people (peers, tutors or colleagues) may have an opportunity to question and challenge your views.

Reflecting with peers

Seeing what you have observed through the lens of *peers'* perspectives can be interesting as they may have quite different interpretations. Just like you, they will bring to the observation certain preconceived ideas and, depending on their backgrounds, they may see different things. Dewey (1997b), in his writing, uses the example of various experts all viewing a horse slightly differently depending on their specialisms. The horse trader, jockey and zoologist, each with their particular frame of reference based on experience, see the same horse in terms of making a deal, winning a race or classifying the species. Similarly, people may read and judge the observation in Vignette 9.1 differently, depending on their backgrounds. A sports coach, a parent of a child of a similar age, a play worker or a practitioner who works with toddlers in a day nursery may all have varying opinions. For example, the day nursery practitioner may praise the attention to the child's safety, while the play worker might feel frustrated by the overprotective parenting that limits the child's independence. You do not have to accept all of your peers' opinions, but they may provide useful insights and new angles, helping you to reflect more deeply on what you have observed.

In addition to interrogating your own viewpoint and challenging your interpretations of the child's behaviour, your peers may also give you feedback on how effectively you have communicated what you observed. The person who reads your observation can only see what you have written. They are unlikely to know the child or the wider context, so their reactions and questions may reveal limitations of the recorded observation. For example, if Adam's scream was clearly one of excitement and not frustration or fear then there is an indication that you could improve your skills in using appropriately descriptive language. Comparing the impressions that readers have gained with the information that you aimed to convey will give you insights into the effectiveness of your observation record. Discussions may also focus upon the chosen method of observation and your peers may offer suggestions for alternative approaches.

Reflecting with practitioners or parents

If you are a practitioner-student and your observations also form part of your regular duties, you will have the opportunity to reflect on your observations with colleagues. If you are a student, who has conducted the observation either in an early years setting or at home, you may also seek to reflect with other people involved in the observations. You might have already agreed to share only your written observation record (e.g. the content of the left-hand column of Vignette 9.1), but not your own reflections, feelings and thoughts (shown in the second column). The position you take, during discussions with practitioners or parents, is to listen and learn from their points of view. Such discussions are only for your own learning and must not be used for any other purposes by anyone (as discussed in Chapter 5).

Reflecting in the light of theory

The fourth lens, that of *theory*, can also provide a focus for reflection on your own, with peers, and/or parents/practitioners. Sharing ideas about the theoretical perspectives that might be important for understanding the observation and making suggestions, based upon what you and others have read, can provide a foundation for writing about your observations for assignments (see Chapter 13). In preparation and during shared reflections you can add points about relevant theory in the reflective notes alongside your observation record (see Figure 9.2) or in your Learning Diary. A discussion about which theorists' views are supported or contradicted by evidence from an observation can also be an exciting way of developing knowledge of theory.

Observation record (Description of sensory information)	Reflections on observation (Observer's thoughts and feelings with theory notes added) included in the Learning Diary
Adam (aged 22 months), who has just woken up, runs over to the slide in his back garden making babbling noises. As he approaches the slide Adam grips on to the ladder with both hands and lifts his legs up off the ground. Adam then pulls himself up the ladder to the top of the slide, assisted by his mother. She then picks Adam up, as he approaches the top of the slide, and helps him to sit down. Adam starts to scream loudly. His mother holds on to him while he slides down the slide. Adam laughs and babbles as he slides down and approaches the bottom of the slide.	Full of energy after his sleep

Read about benefits of rest and sleep for young children

Gaining strength in arms and legs – can coordinate climbing slide steps

Check Mary Sheridan for normative stages of physical development – climbing steps

Is this the best way of supporting him?

Vygotsky – ZPD; Bruner - scaffolding

Does he scream because he doesn't like being at this height or because he wants to do this independently?

Mood changes quickly back to positive one. |

Figure 9.2 Form showing reflective and theoretical notes of the observation excerpt from Vignette 9.1

As Drummond (1998:100) suggests: 'Our own observations can illuminate the work of psychologists, researchers and educators. As we watch and listen, their work seems less remote, academic or theoretical: the children bring it to life.'

Considering the child's perspective in reflection

The child's experience and perspectives should be central to all four lenses of reflection. Observers should constantly think and attempt to understand what it is like to be a child of a particular age, in a specific setting and under certain circumstances. This will enable them to develop an empathetic view of the child's experience. For example, how does it feel to be a small boy learning to use a slide, managing to climb up the ladder, manoeuvring his body at the top and the brief thrill of the descent? How does it feel to have adult support, reassuring to be kept safe or frustrating not to be able to slide independently? A group can engage in discussion of their different impressions of what the child's experience might be. The phrase *'Adam starts to scream loudly'* may be open to a dialogue and discussion of the possible interpretations of this statement: is he scared, excited, frustrated? This may lead to insights about his experience, which are rooted in the collective and negotiated understanding of what it is like to be Adam.

Utilising Brookfield's four lenses of reflection and keeping in mind the child's perspective is helpful at different levels. First, you can start formulating initial ideas to be examined through systematic analysis and interpretation of your observational records (to be discussed in Chapters 10 and 11). Second, as a student, reflection provides the basis for understanding your own learning and for developing professional skills (to be discussed in Chapter 14). Third, if you already work with young children, or plan to do so in the future, reflection can play an important part in making decisions about children's care and education and can also contribute to your own professional development.

Summary

In this chapter we have explored individual and group approaches to reflection on observations. Based on Dewey's and Piaget's views of knowledge construction and on ideas from Schön and Gibbs we suggested reflection as a basis for making meaning from observation. We considered Brookfield's four lenses of reflection and reiterated the centrality of the observer's commitment to the child. Insights from reflective discussions would be informative for the systematic analysis of the observations, discussed in the next chapter.

Concluding activity

Having read this chapter, revisit your first observation record and reflect on how you might have done it differently.

Chapter 10
Analysis of observation records

In this chapter we focus on the systematic analysis of observation records. We discuss the steps involved in the analysis, ways of coding and filing analysed data and different kinds of presentation of data. We summarise key principles of analysis and highlight some of its challenges and limitations.

Vignette 10.1

Observation record (Description of sensory data)	Reflections on observation (Feelings, thoughts and relevant theory)
Raya sits in front of a box with sensory resources (treasure basket). She picks up objects one at a time; looked at them, waved them, listened to them and placed them next to her. She chatted to herself. Words were mainly unrecognisable. Occasionally I recognised words such as ball, box, key.	Interesting resources have been provided. Is Raya familiar with them?
All her chatter was (very) animated with a range of intonation.	Inferential statement – my judgement about the situation!
She moved on to playing with objects together in the basket. She picked up the pan, put the metal whisk in the pan and then tried other metal objects together. She tried to put the wooden whisk into the pan. It didn't fit. She went back to emptying and investigating objects (randomly) one at a time.	Is this the beginning of pretend play? Is it really randomly?
Raya left the treasure basket then quickly returned and continued emptying more objects from the treasure basket one at a time. She then started reading the mini-book to herself. When she finished reading the book she said 'Bye bye book'.	Why is a book in a treasure basket? Need to find out more about the treasure basket. How does it contribute to young children's developmental skills?
She continued emptying objects one at a time from the basket. Each time she chatted to herself (as if explaining what she had got or was doing).	These are my interpretations of the situation, but not sure this is what is actually happening!
She put the book in the treasure basket. Then put the other objects back in the basket, chatting to herself (as if she was naming objects as she did it).	
Raya left the activity and went to play in the home corner.	

Introduction

The vignette above is an adapted observation record from a research study conducted with the aim to observe and record the range of developmental skills demonstrated by young children when playing with the treasure basket (Papatheodorou 2010a). Raya, who at the time was two years and two months old, was observed for 20 minutes (the duration of her play with the treasure basket) playing on her own. This was one of the first observations of the study which the observer began to analyse.

As suggested in previous chapters, the observer has written up the observation record, by separating sensory data from inferential statements (dark shaded statements in the vignette) and reflected on the observation (light shaded statements). These are important initial processes of starting to make sense of the observation. The systematic and methodical analysis of the observation, however, is a distinct process that starts after the observation record is written up and it focuses on factual data (Delamont 2002). Analysis as a systematic and methodical process adheres to general key principles and guidelines and, depending on the purpose and specific questions of the observations, employs particular strategies and techniques. In this chapter we show the process by making reference to Vignette 10.1.

What is analysis?

The term analysis (from the Greek verb αναλύω) means I take apart the constituent elements or segments of a thing, phenomenon or event. For the analysis of data, such as observation, this means that 'we try to discern the smallest elements into which something can be reduced and still maintain meaning if lifted out of the immediate context and then discover relationships between those elements' (Ely et al. 1997:161). Each of these smallest elements or analytical segments should then be sorted out into categories which, in turn, are clustered into themes. Themes are statements of meaning related to particular concepts and ideas (Piaget 2002/1926; Ely at al., 1997). This process of analysis is known as *content* analysis (Sommer and Sommer 1986). Theory box 10.1 shows how Piaget applied this system of analysis to his observations of children's language.

Theory box 10.1

Excerpt from Piaget's description of his analysis

Once the material was collected, we utilized it as follows. We began numbering all subjects' sentences. As a rule the child speaks in short sentences interspersed with long silences or with the talk of other children. Each sentence is numbered separately. Where the talk is a little prolonged, the reader must not be afraid of reckoning several consecutive sentences to one number, so long as to each sentence containing a definite idea only one number is affixed. In such cases, which are rare enough, the division is necessarily arbitrary, but this is of no importance for statistics dealing with hundreds of sentences.

Once the talk has been portioned out into numbered sentences, we endeavour to classify these into elementary functional categories.

Piaget (2002:6-7)

Translating this definition into practical actions means that when you analyse your observational records, you break them into phrases that contain specific information and/or represent a particular concept (see Appendix 2 for the segmented observation record of Vignette 10.1). To establish categories and themes, you will need to return to the aims and specific questions of your observations; these will provide you with a starting point (Delamont 2002). If you have conducted an observation with the aim of recording the range of a young child's developmental skills (as in the vignette above), you may have in mind, from your previous readings, certain categories and themes that you expect to find in your observations. This process is known as *literature-based* analysis (Auerbach and Silverstein 2003; Dey 1993).

If the aim of your observation is open ended, for instance, *what does a child do and how does s/he play with a treasure basket*, you may start forming your categories from your observations. You will need to think about the relevance and meaning of your analytical segments with regards to the child's doing, look at their relationships and cluster them into categories. You then organise them under emerging broader themes that they may relate to, for instance, child development, or play patterns, use of resources etc. This process is known as *open coding* system of analysis (Auerbach and Silverstein 2003; Dey 1993).

In general, when you analyse your observations you can either use *predefined literature-based* categories and themes or you can use an open coding system of analysis, allowing your categories and themes to emerge from your data. In the following sections we exemplify the analysis of the observation record in Vignette 10.1 by using predefined literature-based categories and themes. We will exemplify open coding in Chapter 11.

A step-by-step approach to analysis

There are several steps to be followed for the analysis of your observational data, including: making explicit your theoretical position; adopting an analytical framework; assigning analytical segments to categories; and sorting categories into themes.

Making explicit your theoretical position

The observer in Vignette 10.1 conducted the observation with the particular aim of identifying the developmental skills exhibited by Raya, when she was playing with the treasure basket. To address this aim it was appropriate for the observer to refer to child development theories and find out the potential developmental skills that could be identified in the observation record. These included areas such as: motor development; perceptual development; cognitive development; language development; communication; emotional development; social development; and moral/spiritual development. This theoretical structure then formed the basis for a potential analytical framework that the observer could use to organise the segmented observation record (Ely et al. 1997). The observer positioned her/himself in child development theories.

When you adopt a theory, which informs your analytical framework, you will need to provide a rationale, explaining why it is appropriate to your observations. In case you consider multiple theories you will need to articulate any competing or overlapping ideas and make explicit (i) your choice of theory or (ii) how you have synthesised components and principles of different theories to provide a coherent and well-argued framework that is relevant to the purpose of the observations.

Deciding your analytical framework

In the vignette above, child development theories offered the observer a structure for her/his analytical framework, but its final version was also informed by (i) the insights gained from reflections (individual and with others; in action and on action) and (ii) the content of the observational record. The observer considered ideas that emerged from reflections and read and re-read the observational

Table 10.1 A predefined literature-based initial analytical framework

Predefined literature-based themes	Predefined literature-based categories
1. Motor development	Gross motor skills
	Fine motor skills
2. Language development	Single words
	Combination of words
	Full sentences
	Other (to be specified)
3. Communication	Verbal
	Non-verbal
4. Cognitive development	Exploration
	Problem solving
	Sorting
	Other (to be specified)
5. Emotional development	Expressing emotions
	Responding to emotions
6. Social development	Pro-social skills
Other emerging themes (Other)	Other (to be specified)

record to become familiar with its content. Through this process the observer created an initial analytical framework as shown in Table 10.1. This included six developmental themes that each consisted of a number of relevant categories and an additional theme for unanticipated emerging categories.

Assigning categories

The observer read the observation record again and assigned each analytical segment (shown in Appendix 2) to a relevant category. New categories were created for analytical segments that did not fit the initial framework. This process led to a revised analytical framework shown in Table 10.2 (new categories are shown in shaded rows). This updated version of the analytical framework could then be used for the analysis of subsequent observations.

Table 10.2 A revised analytical framework

Revised literature-based themes	Revised literature-based categories
Motor development	Gross motor skills
	Fine motor skills
Language development	Single words
	Combination of words
	Full sentences
	Self-talk
	Self-talk/Unrecognisable words
	Self-talk/Recognisable words
	Full sentences/Self-talk
Communication	Verbal
	Non-verbal
Cognitive development	Exploration
	Exploration/Visual, kinetic and auditory
	Problem solving
	Sorting
	Combining objects
	Encountering problems
	Looking for solutions
	Cognitive shift?
Emotional development	Expressing emotions
	Responding to emotions
Social development	Pro-social/Sense of order
	Pro-social/Independence
Other emerging themes – Perceptual	Attention?
Other emerging themes – Not developmental	Age

Sorting out categories – keeping things in a state of flux

Analytical segments assigned to the same category were then brought together to find how they relate with each other, question their assumed relationships, refine the categories and start formulating some ideas. For example, the analytical segments *'She picks up objects one at a time'* and *'She continued emptying objects one at a time from the basket'* (see Appendix 2) were assigned to the category of *fine motor skills*.

The identification of initial categories however, may not be the final ones. The observer needs to keep things in a state of flux. For example, the observer found that some segments could not be assigned to clear categories. The analytical segment *'She then started reading the mini-book to herself'* was assigned to two different categories: *Other – attention?* and *Other – cognitive shift?* (see Appendix 2). The question mark demonstrated the observer's ambiguity as to whether the book distracted Raya from what she was doing or whether she found in the book something that was relevant to her previous activity. Such ambiguities may be clarified by examining this segment in relation to the content of the whole observation record and/or by revisiting ideas explored in reflections. Sometimes ambiguities may be carried forward to be explored during the analysis of subsequent observations.

Clearly, analysis is not a linear process. You will need to visit and revisit your segmented document (in Appendix 2) and the observation record in its totality, and take into account ideas from initial reflections (shown in Vignette 10.1) and allow for further reflections. You need to continue with this process until you reach a point where you feel that potential options for sorting analytical segments have been exhausted and you are satisfied with the final categories and themes that you have created.

Managing data – coding, indexing and filing

For the analysis of one observation record only, it may be easy to remember and organise your categories and themes by just keeping notes. For a series of observation records, however, you will need to have a system to manage them. This system includes: coding categories and themes, and indexing and filing them.

Coding

A colour coding scheme may be used, with different colours representing different categories and themes. Alternatively, a coding system may be developed by using meaningful acronyms. For instance, for the above analytical framework, acronyms consisting of two components were assigned to each category shown in Appendix 3. The first component referred to the overall theme or area of development (e.g. MOT for motor development), while the second component of the code was attributed to specific categories within this theme, for example GR for gross motor skills, FI for fine motors skills. So, the code MOT-GR corresponded to motor development-gross motor skills; MOT-FI to motor development-fine motor skills and so on.

Analytical segments that formed a new category were given a new code. For example, she *"Looked at them, waved them, listen to them and placed them next to her"* (a new category referring to *Cognitive - Visual, kinetic and auditory exploration*) was assigned a new code COGN-EXPL/VKA (see appendix 3). Similarly, *"Raya is two years and one month old"* (a new category referring to non-developmental information) was coded OTHER-Not developmental information to accommodate this category. A potential coding system for the analysis of subsequent observations is shown in Appendix 3 (shaded rows show the new codes).

Coding can be done either by hand or by using an appropriate computer program. The latter is particularly useful for large sets of observations or any other textual and written data. It is quick and flexible, but it cannot replace the thinking behind the coding. The thinking is done by the observer. Therefore, as Delamont (2002) suggests, even if you intend to use appropriate software, it is important that you start with some coding done by hand. Coding is not an end in itself; instead it is a useful tool for examining and re-examining the observational data (Richards 2005).

One way of working by hand is to use one copy of observation records to show all categories. This can be done by making notes on the margins or on a separate column (as shown in Appendix 2) and/or use 'stick-on' notes and tags to label and code each category. Another way is to make multiple copies of the observation record and identify one category or theme on each sheet (Delamont 2002).

Indexing and filing

Whatever the system of coding, you will need to file your data in a meaningful way and for easy access. For example, if you want to access all data that refers to cognitive development you should have placed all relevant categories in a file, folder or envelope under the same title. If appropriate, especially for large sets of data, you may have sub-files for each coded category.

Presentation of analysed data

Once you have analysed all your observations, you will need to organise and present your categories and themes in a meaningful way. This can be done by using words and sentences (qualitative presentation) and/or by using numbers (quantitative presentation). Whatever the format of the presentation of your data, it is important that it provides a coherent account. Table 10.3, for instance, tells us that Raya displayed fine motor skills; her language was mainly self-talk, including recognisable and unrecognisable words and full sentences; her cognitive skills were demonstrated in visual, kinetic and auditory exploration, combining and sorting objects, encountering problems, looking for solutions, problem solving and cognitive shift; she expressed emotions and pro-social skills such as sense of order and independence; there was also a question of distracted attention.

If you need to quantify your observational data, then you may tally each category and calculate their appearance within each dimension (third and fourth column in Table 10.3). You may present them summatively as in Table 10.4 or in a pie chart or bar chart (Figures 10.1 and 10.2, respectively).

Key principles and basic rules of analysis

You will have appreciated by now that the analysis of observational data is an ongoing and continuous process that requires principled and disciplined thought, demonstrated in the explicitness of (i) your theoretical position and analytical framework and (ii) the logical processes, as well as identification of any inconsistencies emerging from your analysis (Richards 2005; Delamont 2002; Sommer and Sommer 1986).

Analysis involves at least three interlinked phases, as follows.

1. *The preliminary phase* starts with conducting and recording accurate and detailed observations, differentiating factual from inferential statements, followed by individual and group reflections to sketch out initial ideas, and make links with extant literature or locate additional and/or new literature.

Table 10.3 Qualitative and quantitative presentation of analysed observational data

Area of development	Observed developmental skills during play with a treasure basket – Qualitative	Tally frequencies	Frequency
Motor development	Fine motor skills	III	3
Language development	Self-talk	III	
	Self-talk/Unrecognisable words	I	
	Self-talk/Recognisable words	I	
	Self-talk/Full sentences	I	6
Cognitive development	Visual, kinetic and auditory exploration	I	
	Problem solving	I	
	Sorting	I	
	Combining objects	I	
	Encountering problems	I	
	Looking for solutions	I	
	Cognitive shift	I	7
Emotional development	Expressing emotions	I	1
Social development	Sense of order	I	
	Independence	I	2
Other emerging themes	Distraction of attention	I	1
	Not developmentally related information (Age)		1

2. *The systematic analysis phase* starts after the completion of the observations and involves several steps and actions:

   - reading and re-reading each observation and all observations in their totality to re-engage with the initial ideas and insights elicited from reflections;

   - stating explicitly the analytical framework and the theoretical position adopted;

   - breaking down observations into small, meaningful segments;

Table 10.4 Summative presentation of developmental skills

Areas of development	Frequency
Motor development (MOT)	3
Language development (LANG)	6
Cognitive development (COGN)	7
Emotional development (EMOT)	1
Social development (SOC)	2
Other (OTHER)	2

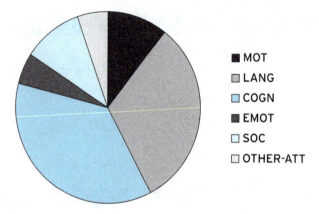

Figure 10.1 Pie chart showing developmental skills

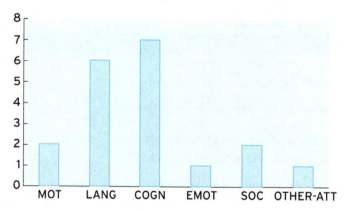

Figure 10.2 Bar chart showing developmental skills

- creating as many categories as possible and ceasing only when they start to overlap with each other or saturate;

- ensuring flexibility to accommodate emerging categories and themes;

- assigning observation segments to categories;

- sorting categories;

- combining categories reflecting similar ideas and concepts;

- organising categories under the themes of your analytical framework;

- ensuring that you pay as much attention to unexpected, inconsistent and conflicting data as you do to repeated patterns and similarities; inconsistent data can be telling and provide alternative perspectives of looking at observed individuals;

- coding and filing your analysed data in a meaningful way for easy retrieval.

(See Figure 10.3.)

3. *The data presentation phase* involves the organisation of emerging themes and categories and their presentation either qualitatively (in phrases, words, concept maps and diagrams) and/or quantitatively (frequencies, pie charts or bar charts). How the data will be presented depends on the purpose and questions of your observation. It is important however to remember the presentation of your data gives you and your readers a coherent account that portrays known concepts and ideas and/or introduces new ones.

Challenges and limitations

Analysis of data presents challenges and has its own limitations. The initial identification of categories is fraught with ambiguity and uncertainties and it is particularly challenging for novice observers. In addition, while some categories such as those describing factual and structural components/elements of observations may be easier to be established, others such as inferential or more subjective categories related for example to emotions, moods, affect etc. may be more difficult to substantiate. Finally, this kind of analysis only describes the content of observations (e.g. an observed child's communications, actions and interaction) but not why they are that way (Richards 2005; Sommer and Sommer 1986).

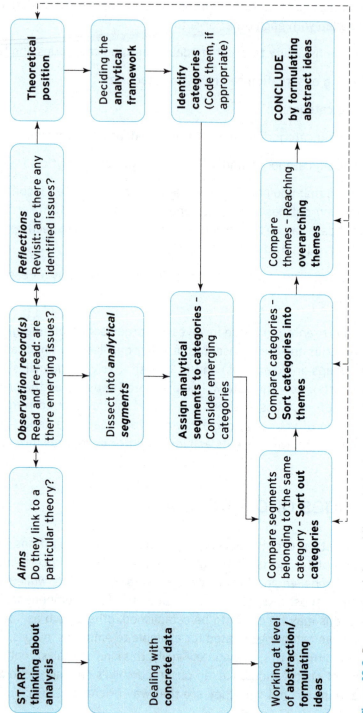

Figure 10.3 Processes and steps of the analysis of observation records

Evidently, although there are key principles and basic rules for the analysis of observation, there are no certainties and assurances. You will need to address any uncertainties and complexities you experience in a systematic and reasoned manner. You will need to be able to explain what you did, how you did it and why. This will give you the skill and confidence you need for data analysis. Sara Delamont (2002:184) reminds us that 'There is no need to be frightened of analysis. It only needs systematic attention to the data, the wide reading already going on, and a bit of self-confidence.'

Summary

In this chapter we discussed data analysis as an ongoing, continuous, principled and disciplined process. We outlined the steps involved in the analytical process, considered a system of coding and filing data and suggested ways of presenting them in a meaningful way. We summarised key principles underpinning analysis and considered some of the challenges and limitations. We noted that while analysed data tells us about the content of the observation records, they tell us very little about their meaning. This issue will be discussed in the next chapter.

Concluding activity

Re-analyse the observational excerpt in Vignette 10.1 to establish different types of play shown by Raya when playing with the treasure basket. You should develop a literature-based analytical framework informed by theories of play.

Chapter 11
Interpretation of child observation

In this chapter we focus on the interpretation of analysed observational data, that is, how observers understand and make sense of their findings and communicate them to others in a well-substantiated and meaningful way. More specifically, we will discuss the complex and reciprocal roles of initial analysis and interpretation that require continuous reflection.

Vignette 11.1

Presentation of initial categories and themes emerging from the analysis of Vignette 10.1

Area of development	Categories of developmental skills observed during play with a treasure basket
Motor development	Fine motor skills
Language development	Self-talk
	Self-talk/Unrecognisable words
	Self-talk/Recognisable words
	Self-talk/Full sentences
Cognitive development	Visual, kinetic and auditory exploration
	Problem solving
	Sorting
	Combining objects
	Encountering problems
	Looking for solutions
	Cognitive shift
Emotional development	Expressing emotions
Social development	Sense of order
	Independence
Other emerging themes	Distraction of attention
	Not developmentally related information (Age)

Introduction

In Chapter 10, we discussed analysis as a continuous process that helps the observer to identify the emerging categories in a systematic way. This analytic process informs the observer about the *content* of the observations, but it reveals very little about the meaning of observations. For instance, what do these categories tell us about the individuals and the phenomena we observe? Are there relationships between categories, and what new ideas and concepts could we form from them? This chapter is about how we interpret observations.

Interpretation

The interpretation of observations requires that the observer shifts attention from *content analysis* to *thematic analysis*, attempting to explore the meaning and essence of the emerging key themes. The general principle is that thinking moves from the concrete descriptive data to general themes that encompass as much of the data as possible and have transferable meaning in conceptual terms. Interpretation takes observers beyond where they were or what they knew when they started the observations, and it enhances and extends thinking in different ways. It helps them to understand the observed child in the light of known theories and literature; eases them into ways of finding new perspectives of seeing and understanding the observed in her/his context; and extends initial ideas and may even develop new theories. In interpretation, it is not the findings (e.g. categories and themes) of the observations that are significant, but the way they are interpreted and the meaning given to them (Peacock cited in Ely et al. 1997).

Interpretation is a meticulous, thorough and painstaking process that starts with the initial analysis of the observational records and continues with further reflections on these findings which, in turn, may trigger additional analysis. It is a process whereby the observer circles around, and criss-crosses all the information that has accumulated. As the interpretation process starts, the observer goes back and forth from findings to the whole observation record and notes included in the Learning Diary. These are then interrogated in the light of the purpose and specific questions of the observations and the theoretical position adopted, in order to consider and reconsider possible alternative meanings.

It is complicated to have so much data, so the task of interpretation is to distil key concepts and ideas portrayed in the findings which, when contextualised, are meaningful to a wider informed audience (Atkinson 1989). Thus, observers gradually narrow the focus of the analysis to the most salient and prevalent themes. They may engage in further in-depth analysis to refine, combine and recombine categories and/or themes in order to tease out key meanings and reach broader encompassing themes that have significant factual or emotional impact (Ely et al. 1997).

For example, in Vignette 11.1, the observer initially sorted the emerging categories using a child development framework, but through further reflection some of the categories were regrouped or collapsed to create some new and more meaningful categories. For instance, examining the categories *Encountering problems*, *Looking for solutions* and *Problem solving* (within the cognitive theme) in the light of the full observation record, the observer realised that all these behaviours occurred during certain play activities. As a result these categories were regrouped into a new category that conceptualised problem solving as a multiple-component process rather than as a distinct separate category (Figure 11.1). On the basis of this new insight the observer conducted further literature searches to find out more about the concept of problem solving.

Similarly, looking at the categories of *Self-talk/Unrecognisable words*, *Self-talk/Recognisable words* and *Self-talk/Full sentences* (in the *Language development* theme) and re-examining them in the light of the actual observational record, it became clear that self-talk was the key feature rather than the number of words spoken. These categories were then collapsed into a new category of *Self-talk* that reflected Vygotsky's (1986) concept of inner speech with which the observer was familiar (Figure 11.2).

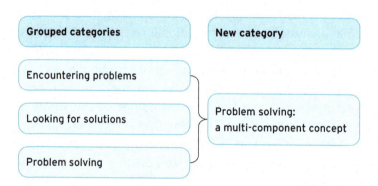

Figure 11.1 Grouping categories – creating a new category

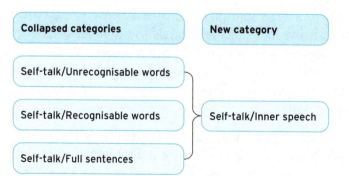

Figure 11.2 Collapsing categories – creating a new category

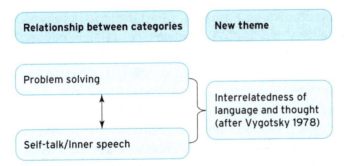

Figure 11.3 Finding relationships between categories – establishing a new theme

Revisiting the original observation record, the observer realised that *Self-talk/Inner speech* appeared along side actions that related to *Problem solving*. The relationship between these two categories was then conceptualised into an overarching theme that portrayed a key concept of child development theories, that is, the interrelatedness between language and thinking (Vygotky 1986) (see Figure 11.3). Through this process, the observer was able to identify known concepts even in this short observational record and to explore new ideas. Equally important, the observer was able to understand the mental processes behind the child's actions and her persistent engagement for over twenty minutes. Ultimately, when interpreting observations, it is not the findings alone that are significant but the issues they raise and the meanings we give to them.

The role of theory

The interpretation of findings requires prior knowledge of the particular academic discipline that informs the study, as it offers the lens through which we interrogate and interpret observations. For instance, in the analyses and interpretations of the observational record in Vignette 10.1, the observer relied on her knowledge of Vygosky's (1978) theory about the development of language and thought to find relationships and give meaning to the findings. The concept of problem solving as a multiple component process led the observer to search for new relevant literature that was located in the field of medical education, where the concept has been extensively researched. Therefore, although knowledge of relevant theories and literature is intrinsic to the whole process, the observer should be alert and consider other theories that may emerge (Ely et al. 1997).

Observers should also be aware that initial theories may become strait-jackets, where they may try to fit findings, resulting in missing incongruent data that may be of critical significance. Therefore, while a clearly articulated theoretical position is useful to set boundaries to observations, it is important that observers are prepared to critique and, if appropriate, to challenge earlier frameworks on the basis of findings. Unquestioning adoption of theories and predetermined conclusions are unhelpful, because 'no theory in science is final' (Donaldson 1978:9). Observations can be a means of recognising familiar ideas and understanding their key principles (e.g. inner speech and thinking). They can also be a means of formulating new ideas or seeing them from a different perspective (e.g. problem solving as a multi-component process).

Purpose and meaning

The aims and questions of observations are crucial in the analytical and interpretation process. They help the observer to hone in on the principal dimensions on which the analysis is based. Sometimes, however, narrow or poorly articulated questions may 'cut off and stifle critical and creative thinking' (Ely at al. 1997:236). They can predetermine answers that stem from and/or fit neatly within particular theories and observations can become more of a tick-box exercise. The interpretation process does not discard either the aims or the initial analysis, rather it builds on them. It expands thinking and poses a range of possibilities and alternative views. It takes the observer beyond what s/he previously knew, and it may refine and sharpen initial questions possibly leading to alternative or multiple analytical frameworks.

Using multiple analytical frameworks

Alternative and/or multiple analytical frameworks are usually used when (i) observations are conducted with broad purposes, (ii) reflections on the initial analysis point towards alternative theoretical perspectives, and (iii) observations are guided by more than one research question. Vignette 11.2 exemplifies the use of multiple analytical frameworks that were adopted because of the broad focus of the observation, the subsequent analysis undertaken as a result of further reflections on the initial findings, and the additional question posed.

Vignette 11.2

Excerpt from an observational record

Ms Maya asked all the children to sit round. She was going to tell them about special clothes that people wear for special jobs. Jake stood at the back and then he sat down. He looks at a late arrival. He sat with his legs stretched out in front of him, not cross-legged like most others. Jake pulled at the neck of his T-shirt and then fiddled with his shoes. One boy smiled at him. Jake did not smile back. He moved around and sat sideways looking round the room.

Ms Maya was asking who wore the clothes in the picture she was holding up. No one replied. She asked again what the clothes were. 'A coat and a mask', said Jake. Ms Maya appeared not to hear him. 'Do you know who wears these?', she asked again. 'A doctor', said Jake quietly. Ms Maya did not appear to hear him. 'A doctor', she said. 'The clothes are a coat and a mask.' 'I know that', said Jake.

Observer's initial reflections

To this point of doing my observation, I felt sorry and disappointed that Jake's replies to questions had apparently not been heard, and I thought he must have been having the same sort of feelings. My personal feelings and response reminded me of Laishley's (1987:73) statement: 'A child who has not had the respect of an adult's attention is less likely to learn to attend well . . . in turn.'

Emerging overarching themes

Analysis I: focuses on the child's experience (see Figure 11.4)	Analysis II: focuses on practice/pedagogy (see Figure 11.5)
Jake, the 'ideal' pupil, shifted his attention to off-task behaviours, due to teacher's non-reciprocated interaction	The teacher focused on information transmission, but Jake learned to negotiate his social space, due to teacher's non-reciprocated interaction

Vignette 11.2 comes from a series of non-participant observations of a four-year-old boy in a nursery class. The observations were conducted in weekly sessions of one hour's duration over a period of ten weeks, and they started four weeks after Jake joined the nursery class. The aim of the observations was to find out: What is Jake doing in his nursery class? The excerpt above is part of the first observation that took place during 'carpet time'. Ms Maya, the adult in charge, and all the children in the nursery class, 22 in total, were present.

The observer first segmented the observational record and identified initial categories. The initial sorting of categories and themes led to an analytical framework that related to *child-adult interactions* within a classroom (Figure 11.4). Having established the view that Jake is the 'ideal' conforming and responsive pupil, the observer concluded that the teacher's non-reciprocal interaction diverted his attention to inappropriate behaviours. Further reflections on the initial categories and their conceptualisation and comments from peers (e.g. *how feasible was it for a teacher to acknowledge each and all children's individual responses in a class of 22*) led the observer to reconsider the emerging categories and regroup them with theories of pedagogical practice informing a second analytical framework (Figure 11.5). The second analysis revealed that while instructions and guidance were directed towards the whole class, responses were expected from individual children. The size of the class of 22 children made immediate reciprocal interaction with individual children a challenging task, evidenced by the fact that the teacher was unable to acknowledge Jake's responses. As a result, while the teacher focused on knowledge transmission (knowledge of which Jake was already aware), Jake diverted his attention to off-task behaviours, engaging with peers, whom he previously ignored, to establish rapport with them and learn to work his social space.

The question raised is: is Jake the ignored and neglected child (first analysis) or the resourceful and resilient child (second analysis)? The observer continued the analysis of her further nine observations against both analytical frameworks, aiming to reach some meaningful abstract conclusions in relation to the question *'What is Jake doing in his nursery class?'*

The basics of interpretation

Awareness of the role of initial ideas, impressions and reflections on systematic analysis and interpretations of observations is well established, but vigilance is needed to ensure that they do not take over. Equally, initial insights should not be sidelined for the sake of tidy and uncomplicated analyses and interpretations (Ely et al. 1997). There is a reflective mode in interpretation, where you attempt to give meaning to your observations through your own beliefs, knowledge and experience. You will also need to distance yourselves from this reflective mode, so that you can communicate your experience in a meaningful way that resonates with the knowledge and experience of your audience (e.g. tutors, peers, practitioners, readers). These elements of the analytical and interpretation process need to be carefully weighed in order to reach sound and well-substantiated conclusions.

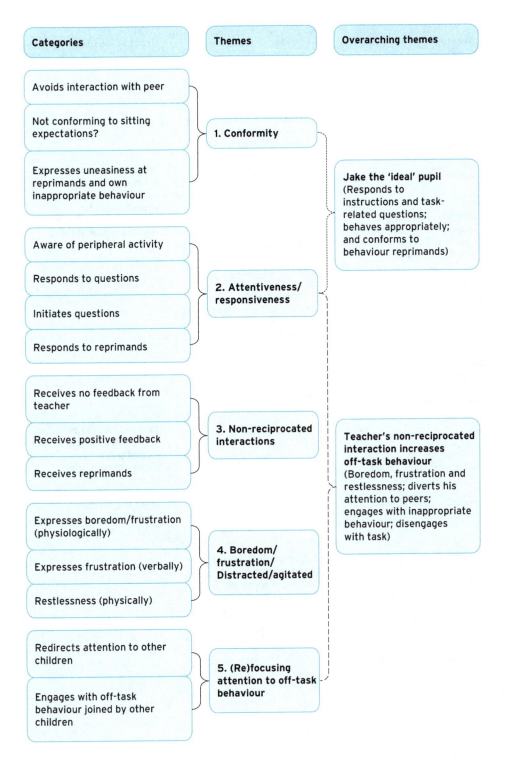

Figure 11.4 An example of emerging categories and themes, using an analytical framework informed by adult-child interaction theories

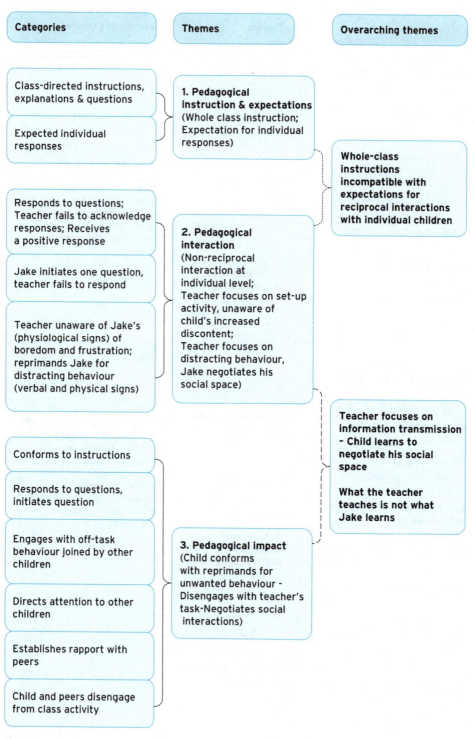

Figure 11.5 An example of emerging categories and themes, using a different analytical framework informed by theories of pedagogy

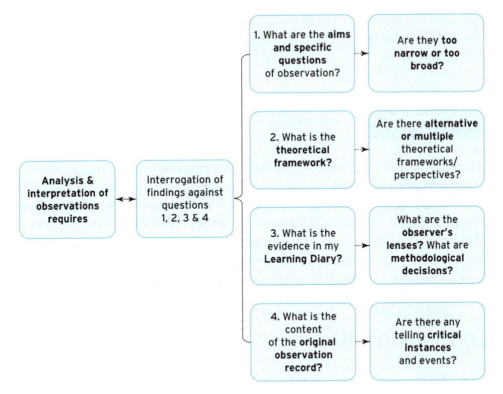

Figure 11.6 The reciprocal process of analysis and interpretation of observations

Interpretation requires that you interrogate your findings against the following (see Figure 11.6):

1. The aims and questions of the observations. Is the focus of observations clear? Are your questions too narrow or too broad? Do you need to refine, reshape and reword them?

2. The adopted and/or emergent theoretical frameworks. Are there alternative or multiple frameworks informed from different areas of study?

3. The Learning Diary (reflective and methodological notes). What are your personal and professional attitudes? Have you been too deeply emerged in the setting? Have these issues coloured your observer lenses? Are there tensions between the non-participant and professional roles? Were there any ethical dilemmas? Were there any challenges when analysing observations?

4. The original observation record. Are there any critical instances and events that give particular meaning to analytical segments and emerging categories and themes?

This is not an exhaustive list of questions to be asked. Observers may ask further or different questions, depending on the specific aim, focus and context of their observations.

Summary

In this chapter we have discussed analysis and interpretation as reciprocal and interwoven processes that are subject to continuous reflections on initial findings. These processes involve interrogation of the findings against the purpose and questions of observations and the theoretical framework adopted. While analysis tells us about the content of observations, it is the interpretation of findings that gives meaning to them, intensifying our understanding of the child, and frames the observation within concepts and abstract ideas.

Concluding activity

Revisit your own observation records and consider whether you can apply a different analytical framework and provide a rationale. Use Figure 11.6 to guide your thinking.

Chapter 12
Observation – a research tool

In this chapter we discuss the uses of observation as a research tool to inform evidence-based practice. We first explore the use of different methods of observation for different purposes and provide a rationale for choosing them. We continue by conceptualising observation as *method* and as *context* by outlining their main philosophical differences and conclude by relating these concepts to debates about qualitative and quantitative research.

Vignette 12.1

Tom, four years old, has been attending the nursery class for two months. When he first joined the nursery school he had difficulty in settling down; he would cry and ask his mother not to leave him in the school and, after her departure, he was constantly at Mary, his key worker's side, holding her hand or skirt. He has now made significant progress. He has stopped crying, he is voluntarily choosing his play activities and he is happy playing on his own. Staff however are concerned that he is isolated and, when playing with other children, he frequently argues and fights with them. Recently he also had tantrums and outbursts for no apparent reason.

Tom's key worker discussed his behaviour with his parents. It was agreed that staff will conduct some observations to (i) establish and monitor the frequency of Tom's arguments, fights, tantrums and outbursts over a period of two weeks; (ii) establish the situations and conditions under which such behaviours occur and (iii) identify the range of his positive and enabling behaviours alongside his challenging behaviours.

Vignette 12.2

Erin Stakis has recently been appointed as the manageress of the Orchard Nursery School. From briefings with her staff she has realised that there is an undercurrent of concern about the physical and relational aggression shown by children in the setting. Staff usually explain such behaviours in the light of the disadvantage experienced by children and their families in the neighbourhood. Notwithstanding the potential impact of the neighbourhood environment, Erin believes that relationships and interactions in peer groups and between children and adults in the nursery school are also important, influencing physical and relational aggressive behaviours. With this in mind, she discussed her ideas with staff. They agreed to address the issue through whole-school pedagogical approaches. They decided to conduct a series of observations over a sustained period of time to find out (i) the nature of interactions and communication within peer groups; (ii) the kinds of relationships with adults; and (iii) the possible factors that inhibit or enable physical and relational aggressive behaviours.

Introduction

The two cases in the vignettes above are rooted in everyday practice, but the nature and extent of concerns and the need for interventions required that information was collected rigorously and systematically, applying research principles (for a definition of research, see Theory box 12.1). In both cases staff decided to conduct a series of observations to address their concerns. The questions raised are: What methods of observation could be used in each case? How would staff decide which methods to use? What would guide their decision? Could the same methods be used in both of the above cases?

Theory box 12.1

What is research?

In daily life, we are constantly involved in research when collecting, comparing and weighing information to make decisions. For example, parents may do their research when choosing their children's schools. Consumers may search for information when deciding on their provider for services such as gas, electricity or internet connection. In this kind of research, however, the degree of system and rigour, when collecting information, would differ from person to person. Some individuals may simply rely on information that is readily available to them without applying any particular process.

Research in social sciences differs markedly from searching for information in our everyday life. It is a disciplined and principled activity. It contributes to the construction of new knowledge that is relevant and meaningful to a particular discipline or field of study. Research is defined as 'systematic, critical and self critical enquiry which aims to contribute to the advancement of knowledge and wisdom' (Bassey 1999:39). It aims 'to arrive at a set of logically interrelated propositions that describe, interpret, explain and/or predict social phenomena' (Sarantakos 1998:9).

Bassey (1999); Sarantakos (1998)

In the following sections of this chapter we address these questions by looking at the methods used by staff in each case and the rationales they provided for their use. This discussion will serve as a springboard to discussing observation as *method* and as *context* with reference to philosophical differences. We conclude by relating this discussion to debates about quantitative and qualitative research.

Observation for research-based practice

In Vignette 12.1 the staff of the nursery school decided to conduct a series of observations to understand Tom's behaviour and provide additional support, if required. They chose to use a checklist to measure Tom's unwanted behaviours; event sampling to collect in-depth information about specific incidents where such behaviours were exhibited; and time sampling to record his overall behaviours at regular intervals throughout the day (for different observation methods, see Chapter 3). Although they had a participant and insider role, the staff decided to take a non-participant role by distancing themselves from the observed child and situations to record information objectively. This information was intended to be communicated to Tom's parents and used as the basis for planning the intervention (see Papatheodorou 2005).

Staff devised a short checklist which consisted of Tom's challenging behaviours that staff intended to measure. The checklist was initially completed by two members of staff. At the end of the first day of observations, the two observers shared their completed checklists to ascertain the degree of agreement of their recordings. Through their discussions, they realised that they had observed and recorded different behaviours and reported different frequency even when they measured the same behaviours. Reviewing their checklists, the observers became aware that the discrepancies in recording were due to the fact that one of them expanded the checklist to include *biting, grabbing toys, pushing children* as distinct behaviours under the item *Other behaviours (specify)* (see Table 12.1). The other observer used the checklist as it was initially devised (see Table 12.2).

The subsequent discussion allowed the observers to think about their own implicit understanding of the behaviours they recorded and provided the opportunity to establish shared definitions of the behaviours under concern. They acknowledged that their understanding and definition of behaviours such as arguments, fights, tantrums and outbursts varied, with the result their records showed different frequency rates. They agreed to establish shared operational definitions to record Tom's behaviour. They defined fights as harming physical actions (e.g. biting, grabbing, pushing, pulling, spitting, hitting) and arguments as verbal and communicative actions (e.g. name calling, bad language, mimicking or disapproving facial expressions to ridicule). On the basis of these understandings they revised the checklist and produced a final version that was used for subsequent observations.

The employment of two observers to complete a checklist independently is one way of establishing reliable and valid observations. The assumption is that

Table 12.1 Checklist completed by A. Alpha (member of staff)

Name: Tom B
Period of observation: 9.00–11.00am
Day 1: 5 November 2009
Observed by: A. Alpha (member of staff)

Behaviours	Free play	Story time	Structured play/activities	Outdoor play	Snack time	Comments
Arguments	III	I	I	I	I	
Fights	II					Tom fights mainly over toys
Tantrums	II					When he can't have the play resources he wants
Outbursts	III		II			
Other behaviour (specify) – biting	II			I		
Other behaviour (specify) – grabbing toys from other children	NN		III	I		
Other behaviour (specify) – pushing children			I	II		

the higher the agreement between two observers the more reliable and objective is the recording of the observations. This *observer inter-agreement* takes place early on in the observational process in order to minimise ambiguities by agreeing operational definitions and criteria that are applied consistently (Sommer and Sommer 1986).

The systematic and rigorous collection of information meant that any planned intervention to address Tom's challenging behaviours was based on reliable evidence. The checklist provided the baseline information for making decisions as to whether an intervention was necessary and, if so, to monitor Tom's behaviour over time. Event sampling offered information about the conditions under which these behaviours occurred, while time sampling placed Tom's challenging behaviour in the context of his other behaviours. The latter information was particularly important in deciding the nature of the interventions to be implemented.

In Vignette 12.2 the staff in the nursery school agreed to conduct a series of observations in order to understand what was going on and find ways that

Table 12.2 Checklist completed by B. Beta (member of staff)

Name: Tom B
Period of observation: 9.00–11.00am
Day 1:   5 November 2009
Observed by: B. Beta (member of staff)

Behaviours	Free play	Story time	Structured play/activities	Outdoor play	Snack time	Comments
Arguments	ℍℍ III	I	I	I	I	Tom plays mainly on his own outdoors
Fights	ℍℍ II			II		
Tantrums	II		I			
Outbursts	II		I			
Other behaviour (specify)						
Other behaviour (specify)						

would be useful for devising appropriate interventions. The methods of observations chosen included narrative observations, video-recordings, tracking maps and sociograms. These methods were deemed appropriate for providing detailed and in-depth information that would allow them to understand the nature of relationships in the nursery school. The staff adopted a participant role, taking an insider perspective. Their perceived knowledge of the neighbourhood and children's lives would help them to make sense of the children's relationships and interactions.

Each member of staff (seven, in total) recorded systematically one observation per day for the duration of one hour, using their preferred method of observation (e.g. narrative, video-recordings, tracking maps or sociograms). In total seven observations were systematically conducted by staff each day, using different observational methods. At the end of each day, inspired by the Reggio Emilia pre-school pedagogical approach (see Edwards et al. 1998), observations were shared among staff for initial reflections in order to explore ideas, examine assumptions and identify areas that might need further sustained observations and systematic recordings.

Initial reflections revealed that observations and discussions captured only adults' views and perspectives. The staff decided to include children in this process during the second week of the project, as they were committed to include children's perspectives and views. Cameras were made available for children to video-record whatever they found interesting or was important to them. Video-snapshots were shared with the children to engage them in discussions in order to illuminate staff understandings of children's experiences.

Observation as method and context

The different uses of observation in the two vignettes above exemplify the employment of observation in two different ways, that is either as a *method* of collecting data and/or as *context* (Angrosino and Mays de Pérez 2003). The distinction of observation as *method* and *context* is an important issue to consider, as it has implications for making judgements about the quality, reliability and truthfulness of the data collected.

When observations are used as a method emphasis is placed on their systematic development and application of methods of observation, and avoidance of bias by removing personal beliefs, values, first impressions and prior knowledge. Observations are expected to elicit data that is reliable and valid. This means that the same findings will be produced if someone else uses the same method of observation to observe the same individual or another population with similar characteristics (Gold cited in Angrosino and Mays de Pérez 2003). In Vignette 12.1 the two observers attempted to distance themselves from the observed child and developed a shared checklist that had a high degree of observer inter-agreement to make their checklist relevant, reliable and valid. The assumption is that when others are using this checklist to record Tom's behaviour they are more likely to arrive at similar findings. This checklist could also be used to record the behaviour of any other child who displays behaviours like Tom's.

The use of observations as *method* assumes collection of data that represents social reality objectively by establishing presumably universal criteria (Glense and Peshkin in Thomas 2003). As a result, it is the quality of the observational record that is important rather than the observation process itself (Angrosino and Mays de Pérez 2003). Such an objectivist approach 'attends to data as real in and of themselves and does not attend the processes of their production' (Charmaz 2006:130). The observer then is relegated to an outsider/non-participant position distinctly separated from the observed individuals (Coulon 1995).

When observation is used as *context* the emphasis is placed on both methods and processes that are supplemented by information about the ways observers interact or enter in a dialogical relationship with the observed individuals (Angrosino and

Mays de Pérez 2003). As we discussed in Chapter 6, the observer, the observed and the setting dynamically interact during observations to create a context of dynamic interactions where the final observation record is located. Observation as *context* emphasises the quality of observations per se and sees observational data and its analysis and interpretation as being created from shared experiences and relationships with participants (Charmaz 2006: Angrosino and Mays de Pérez 2003). Observation as *context* requires the observers to take a participant-insider stance.

Inter-subjectivity is considered significant in the analysis and interpretation of data, when observation is used as *context*. The data may be less systematically collected, but their quality and truthfulness are validated by a systematic and rigorous process of analysis and interpretation involving the observer and the observed. This has been exemplified in Vignette 12.2, where teachers became researchers and expanded their research to include children. It endorses the view that social reality is continuously constructed by all those involved (Coulon 1995).

The uses of observation as *method* or *context* reflect different philosophical views of understanding social phenomena and the world. The first implies an objective social reality, experienced and seen in the same way by all; principles and ideas derived from the observational data have generalised applicability. The latter assumes subjective ways of experiencing and understanding social phenomena; principles and abstract ideas derived from observational data are only meaningful within their particular context, meaning is subjective and con-text bound. These philosophical differences between observation as *method* and *context* resonate to the philosophical differences underpinning quantita-tive and qualitative research (see Theory box 12.2).

Theory box 12.2

Quantitative and qualitative research

The main difference between quantitative and qualitative research is their philosophical assumptions and claims about the social world. Quantitative researchers argue for, and seek to represent phenomena objectively without the interference of the researcher's personal beliefs, values and attitudes. They assume that human beings and social phenomena are influenced and governed by universal laws and principles. Thus, when they collect data, they take steps to maintain neutrality towards the studied individuals and phenom-

▶

ena by using standardised research tools. The data collected is in numerical form and employs statistical methods of analysis (Thomas 2003; Sarantakos 1998). As observers, they adopt a non-participant stance and use standardised checklists, rating scales and tests as methods of collecting data.

Qualitative researchers, on the other hand, maintain that reality is socially constructed and accept that beliefs and attitudes play a mediating role in interpreting and making sense of observed phenomena. They see research as being *value laden* (Denzin and Lincoln 2003). Therefore the aim of research is to provide a clearer and more sophisticated view of social phenomena through methods that withstand disciplined scepticism and critique (Stake 1995). As observers, qualitative researchers take up a participant stance and embrace methods of observation that provide rich and detailed contextualised information. The data collected are in textual, narrative or visual format and are usually content analysed (Thomas 2003).

Denzin and Lincoln (2003); Thomas (2003); Sarantakos (1998) Stake (1995)

Choosing an observation method

An appreciation of the use of observation as *method* or *context* is important to understand, as it allows observers to think about the methods that are appropriate for the aims and specific questions of their observational study. Checklists and rating scales can be used to gather factual information or answer questions that require: measurement (e.g. the frequency of certain behaviours of an individual child or group of children) or comparison (e.g. behaviour differences between, for example, boys/girls, younger/older children). Content-analysed and quantified data from time sampling, event sampling, sociograms, tracking maps and narrative observations can also be used for similar purposes. For instance, content analysis of time sampling in Vignette 12.1 provided information about Tom's range of behaviours as well as their frequency. This allowed staff to make judgements about his overall behaviour. In these instances, the observer maintains neutrality from personal beliefs and attitudes and attempts to minimise her/his impact on the observed individual (observer effect). For these purposes, observation is employed as *method*.

Participant narrative observations and video-recordings are deemed appropriate when the observer wants to understand the behaviour of an individual or group in a particular setting (as in Vignette 12.2). Acknowledging the impact of personal values and insider knowledge (or taking an insider role), these methods can provide data required to address questions of *how* and *why*. In these instances, observation is employed as *context*.

It is possible, however, for observation to be used as both method and context in a single case study (for a definition of a case study, see Theory box 12.3). This happens when phenomena are studied in real-life situations and require holistic understandings and appropriate action to be taken (Yin 2003). For example, in Vignette 12.2, observation was adopted as *context* in order to gain holistic understandings of the relationships in the nursery school and take appropriate action. Some observations, however, provided more contextual data than others. Narrative observations and video-recordings captured detail and in-depth information, whereas sociograms and tracking maps gather factual information about the interactions among children and their movements in the physical space. Even in Vignette 12.1, although staff were committed to examining Tom's behaviour in a neutral and objective way, event sampling (capturing contextual information of events) was employed to understand his behaviour in particular circumstances.

Theory box 12.3

Case study

A case study refers to the study of a contemporary phenomenon in its real-life context, where the researcher has little control of the situation and the boundaries between the phenomenon and context are not clear. A case study usually addresses questions of *how* and *why* and contributes to our knowledge of an individual or a group. It is used in social sciences to contribute to our knowledge in relevant disciplines (e.g. psychology, sociology etc.) and in practice-oriented fields (such as education, social work, architecture etc.) to illuminate decisions taken.

Yin (2003)

The mixing of different methods is usually employed when observers are required to address (i) a range of questions, including questions of *what*, *how many*, and *how* and *why* or (ii) for triangulation purposes, that is, to add rigour, breadth and depth and collect rich data in order to inform their judgements and actions (Yin 2003; Edwards 2001; Bassey 1999; Denzin and Lincoln 2003). To link these ideas to the two vignettes studies above, the staff in Vignette 12.1

used different methods to address different research questions. The staff in Vignette 12.2 used different methods for triangulation purposes, by gathering detail and rich information to illuminate their understanding of the situation and devise appropriate interventions.

Summary

In this chapter we have explored the different uses of observation in real-life situations that require holistic understandings and appropriate actions. We discussed observation as *method* and *context*, referring to different data produced and the role of the observer in each case, and their underpinning philosophical differences. We concluded by considering the use of observation as both method and context in a single case study.

Concluding activity

Revisit the two vignettes above and consider whether you would have used different methods of observation. If so, explain why.

Chapter 13
Writing on child observations

The aim of this chapter is to look at the part that writing plays in the learning process. It offers suggestions for presenting findings from observation in different types of written accounts and considers the sources that an observer could draw on when writing.

> ## Vignette 13.1
>
> *Ellie gets a book from a shelf which is at her eye level. It's a large hard-backed novel with no illustrations. She says, 'We're going to have a story.' She tells a story about a lion and a 'growly monster' with plenty of roars and growls. Puts the book down on the floor and chooses another book. Still a novel, not a children's book. Says, 'This is the unicall one' [unicorn?] 'and roundabouts'. Opens the book and points. 'These are the monsters' pages and these are the unicall pages.' Runs finger along the print and says, as though reading: 'Look unicorn, there's a roundabout. We're just going to it said the Paula mummy.' Shows her mother the book. 'This is your name, look.' Points at the print on the page. 'Do you like my story? I am reading it for you.' Says, 'I got a monster one at my playgroup. There's a lion in another book. If they roar they wake all the children up.' Picks up another book, says, 'Shall I sing my story? You like I sing it?' Runs into the other room and props the book up at the piano. Climbs on to the piano stool. Sits and plays, singing to herself about 'Molly and Polly'.*

Introduction

In presenting an account of what was observed, you have already begun to write. As discussed in Chapter 8, the way that an observation record is presented and the choice of words used are important to give an accurate portrayal of an event to a reader. The vignette above is full of information about one three-year-old-girl's engagement with books in and beyond her home. Like some of the other vignettes in this book, it offers evidence that could be used to create and support written arguments about a child's development and learning. Vignette 13.1 could be used as the basis for writing about the significance of Ellie's use of texts or, more broadly, her speech and language development and/or the various theoretical perspectives that could be used to understand her learning.

Writing offers an exciting opportunity to present findings and interpretations from your observations to other people. Who those other people are, and the type of account that has to be presented to them, will always influence how we write and what is written. Most observers have to write for some form of audience. Student observers will be required to produce assignments based on their observations, which may take the form of essays, learning journals, child studies or research reports. Professionals who observe children may need to produce written reports for parents or perhaps for case review meetings, and researchers will seek to publish, in journals or books, accounts based on the analysis of observational data. Here we consider some aspects of using writing to communicate ideas to others. A short discussion of academic writing is followed by examples of different types.

We have emphasised throughout this book that observation plays a key part in the learning process and so, too, does developing and producing a written text. The whole process of planning, preparing for, carrying out, analysing, interpreting and reflecting on observations is about making meaning and making sense, and this continues when we express ideas in writing. This experience of learning through writing has been emphasised by authors who have written about academic writing from their own experience (see Theory box 13.1). Organising and presenting a piece of writing, based upon your own observations of children, should give you an opportunity to create a unique piece of work that shows your understanding of what you have observed and also your ability to comprehend and apply relevant theory. Writing provides an opportunity to communicate your ideas to other people, so that they can engage with your point of view and perhaps raise questions. Thus written accounts can be the basis for the continuation of the reflective dialogues discussed in Chapter 9.

Theory box 13.1

Why write?

. . . we write primarily because writing is at the heart of our endeavours to reflect, to be thoughtful, to tame and to shape the compost heap of data that is filled with disparate, confusing, and overwhelming raw impressions. Writing helps us to consider, reconsider, plan, replan, make order, check with ourselves and others, and to tell the story of the research in precisely the ways that we feel do justice to it.

Ely et al. (1997:15)

People have different levels of comfort with writing, especially if their work is going to be graded or peer reviewed. In the following section we discuss some types of writing related to students' assessed work. More information about academic writing can be found in a range of textbooks (e.g. Gillett et al. 2009; Murray and Moore 2006; Winter et al. 1999).

Account of an observation

You may be required to write a report on a single observation related to a child's language development. When approaching this form of writing, it is important to begin by deciding how to structure your ideas. If you were to use the observation of Ellie (in Vignette 13.1 above) you could plan your written account like this:

- State focus – to discuss a three-year-old's development of language and literacy.

- Give details of setting (e.g. family home) and participants (e.g. child aged three years one month and adult – child's mother).

- Explain method of observation, reasons for choosing it and description of method with pros and cons (e.g. narrative observation).

- Briefly discuss the content of the observation – include copy as an appendix.

- Discuss the analysis of the observation.

- Discuss and interpret findings (e.g. age-related development; key theories; literacy environment etc.).

- Conclusion and implications of findings for promoting language development.

In a front sheet (shown in Appendix 4) you may also provide summary information about your observations.

Having created this plan, you can begin to draft your written account of the observation in the light of the findings of your analysis and by revisiting your notes (reflective, methodological and theoretical) in your Learning Diary. Look back over lecture notes and related reading and make additional notes, so that you can link evidence from your observation with relevant ideas from literature on the topic. You should then be able to draft a discussion of findings that contains references both to your reading and to your observation. For example, one student has written:

> *There is much in this observation that resonates with Vygotsky's view of cognitive development. Ellie's play and learning are occurring in the social context of her home affected by other social settings, play group and the library, and there is evidence of the cultural tools of books and musical instruments shaping her learning. She constantly uses language to support her play and thinking. Vygotsky (1978) suggests that in play a child might be a head taller than himself – here Ellie plays at activities she may later master, such as reading and playing the piano.*

Following the discussion of findings and key ideas, the conclusion will refer back to the original aim of the observation and summarise the key ideas that emerge from the observation.

Once you have a full draft written, you can begin a process of checking and refining your writing. One way of checking this is to look at each of the paragraphs you have written and highlight the main point in each one. You can then see whether you have included everything. Check that ideas are presented in a logical order, and make sure you have incorporated evidence that supports your arguments. The most important aspect of writing is the clarity of the argument that you are putting forward.

Child study

A common form of writing is a child study, which is based on data from a series of observations (see for example the task set for students in Vignette 4.1). This type of assignment usually requires the observer to describe the observed child, and the contexts in which s/he is growing up, and to discuss her/his development in relation to developmental norms, using information from textbooks and evidence from observations. The following is an example of this type of writing, based upon the opening vignette:

> *'Three-year-olds love to sing and talk' (Mukherji and O'Dea 2000: 49) and Ellie is no exception. Her speech is fluent and expressive with just one mispronunciation (unicall for unicorn) and some syntax errors, which may be evidence of overregularisation of grammatical rules (I got and You like?).*

In order to prepare for this type of writing, it is necessary to analyse all your observations of the child and, through a process of interpretation, decide which salient aspects of your observations you will be discussing and in which order. The identified salient aspects of these observations may focus on areas of development (e.g. physical development, cognitive and language development and social and emotional development) or you could look at development of personality or emergence of sense of humour. Alternatively, the focus could be on different contexts for the child's development, for example showing how Ellie has opportunities for language development in her home, at playgroup and elsewhere; discussing the importance of child-initiated play for her learning; or considering how interactions with adults may support her language development. Whether your focus is the child's development, the environment in which s/he is growing up, or both, it is important to communicate your interest in the life of the child, whom you have observed, to your readers.

There are examples of published child studies that can be read as examples of the genre. Arnold (2003), for example, wrote an account of her grandson's life from the age of eight months to five years linking her observations of his play to theories of child development.

Learning journal

Creating a learning journal, also referred to as a reflective journal, provides an opportunity to write in a more personal style and explore ideas about your own learning as well as about the child. If you are asked to write a learning journal then the notes in your personal Learning Diary will provide a useful basis. The aim of a learning journal is to articulate your own learning journey. This may include information about a range of issues connected to child observation, such as your own experience, exploring theory, and discussing methodological decisions. These are exemplified below. Insights from reflections might provide a useful structure for recording processes of thinking and learning about, and from, observation. In a journal you can make connections between the experiences of the observed child and your own experiences. For example, one student watching recalled her own childhood:

> *From this observation I can see what family life is like in Ruby's family. While conducting the observation I was comparing it to what my family life used to be like. It was quite different, at tea time for example my family would always have dinner at six o'clock and it would be a cooked meal with us all sat around one table. Whereas in Ruby's family the children have dinner and then the parents have dinner later, maybe even after the children have gone to bed.*

The learning incorporated here might be that family routines differ and you need to be open to diverse ways of living. The student who wrote this account has acknowledged the difference from her own experience without making a judgement. Through the process of observing a child within another family you may become more aware of your own attitudes and values.

You can also write in a more personal way about what you have read, linking this to your own experience. For example, a student who had read about Corsaro's (1985) research wrote this response in a learning journal:

Corsaro's (1985) work interested me due to the style in which it was written. It appears from the paper that he 'stumbled' across the idea of researching children's peer culture while undertaking studies with different aims in mind. During my time as a nursery nurse, in various settings, I too enjoyed listening and learning from what children say to each other, and I feel this has been the main appeal to me in reading further into the subject. Corsaro recorded dialogue between children and then, once it was analysed, he found a way of understanding the different ideas of friends and friendships. This is a new concept to me to think about how 'peer cultures' fit in within young children's friendship development and so I want to explore this topic more. His observation method was as a participant observer, I hope to use this same method to create my own research.

The learning displayed here is an explicit linking of theory and experience of practice, in terms of appreciating the value of observing children's informal exchanges, validating an interest in researching friendship, and identifying a useful methodological approach. This last point, about methodology, indicates another key aspect to be covered in a learning journal. It may be important to include reflections on approaches to observations and methods of carrying them out:

All my observations were conducted in the nursery classroom. Amy became immediately aware that I was observing her and initially was very suspicious of me. She would frequently cast her eyes my way to see if I was still 'watching' her. Also, she would behave shyly when she suddenly remembered that I was in the room. For this reason I adapted my role, which initially was that of non-participant, to that of participant observer. I then began participating in the nursery activities and became a member of the nursery group. This certainly worked better as Amy appeared to relax and enjoy my presence and company, which made me feel less conspicuous and more at ease.

This reflects the student's learning about participant roles and, more important, the importance of prioritising the child's well-being in her decision making.

In summary, a learning journal allows the writer to become more self-aware, make sense of their own learning, position themselves as an observer and discuss elements of the observational process. These aspects are important to consider whenever you express views about your overall learning from observations. Whereas these can be made explicit in a learning journal they are important, too, in other forms of writing where awareness of the processes of observing forms a basis for articulating valid and credible arguments.

Research article

In a more structured and formal style of writing, child observations may form all or part of the data of a small-scale research project. The required format will then be similar to a published journal article, with an introduction and discussion of key literature followed by a section describing methodology and the chosen methods of observation and analysis. The findings will then be presented and discussed before arriving at a conclusion that summarises what has been found, in relation to the original research question, and identifies areas for further investigation. Reading a variety of journal articles that give accounts of qualitative research projects will be useful preparation for this type of writing.

A good introduction to a research article will explain the aim of the study, the rationale for undertaking it and the context in which it was carried out. The literature review then demonstrates what is already known about the topic and how the work of other researchers relates to your research questions. How other researchers have conducted their studies may inform your own methodology, depending on your research questions. For example, a student researching the benefits of social play in a nursery classroom discussed Broadhead's (2006) research and was inspired to replicate the methodology, using the 'social play continuum' as a tool to observe and understand the children's imaginative play.

The methodology and methods section of a research report have to be very clear, explaining exactly what was done and justifying the decisions made. Ethical considerations made prior to and during the study should be included, with details of how these were addressed. Information has to be provided about the observed child or children, other participants in the observations and contextual information about where and when the observations were conducted. The methods used should be described with clear reasons for the choice and details of their implementation. The approach to analysing the observation data should also be explained so that the reader can understand the findings and how they were derived.

Findings from the analysis of observations should be presented in a clear and meaningful way. For example, a student who researched children's free-flow play analysed her observations in relation to Bruce's (1991) twelve features of free-flow play and presented the incidences of different features in the form of a chart. The findings should then be discussed in relation to the existing literature. You can highlight insights that are new to you, as a learner, and those which may add to or challenge extant theory and so contribute to knowledge within the field. You can also discuss the strengths and limitations of your observations and the basis on which any claims are made. The conclusion will then summarise the answers that you have found to your research questions and identify directions for further research. If you are a practitioner, the conclusions may also include implications for practice.

Sharing writing

Just as reflection can be enhanced by other people's perspectives so, too, can writing. This can be achieved in different ways, depending on the purpose of the writing. Most writing tasks are demanding and it is beneficial to talk through what you plan to write. You may then be asked questions which help you to develop and explain your written work but, even if that does not happen, speaking about your ideas can help you to clarify your thinking. Once you have begun to write you can show your drafts to other people and invite and welcome their feedback. Sharing your work with somebody else who is working on a similar task may help you both, as you will see the strengths in each other's work and so improve your own. If you show somebody who does not know about your topic they will still be able to comment about how clearly you have put your ideas across and they may also be able to give advice about structure and features of style, spelling, grammar and punctuation.

Another way to work with others and get feedback about your observations and your writing might be to present your writing online, for example as a blog, and invite readers to comment and question. Working together online can also be a useful strategy if you are working with other people to produce a piece of writing such as a group report or shared publication. You can either circulate improved and updated versions of a document by sending them as email attachments or work together on a shared document, which may be hosted on an internal VLE (virtual learning environment) or externally, for example on Google docs.

Summary

In this chapter we have emphasised the part that writing can play in the learning process. We have offered suggestions for presenting findings from observations in different types of written accounts: reports of single observations; child studies; learning journals; and research articles. For all of these the writer is advised to draw upon her/his reflective notes and systematically analysed data from carefully recorded child observations. Through a process of drafting, editing and redrafting, alone and with others (see Theory box 13.2), texts can be produced that demonstrate how child observation has been used to illuminate theory and practice and to answer research questions. As Wolcott (2001:9) reminds us, 'Writing is always challenging and sometimes satisfying'; and we hope you will find writing about your observations a rewarding learning activity.

Theory box 13.2

The process of writing

[It] is a model that has immediate intuitive appeal to adults who write (or avoid writing). For each stage, we can identify different strategies we use. The pre-writing stage is a familiar one. It is identifiable by behaviours such as talking around the subject with colleagues or friends, opening books for inspiration, jotting down ideas . . . Once drafting begins there are all the false starts, the worries about the right tone to adopt . . . Then comes revision which may involve someone else reading what you have written – that can be painful. Then more drafts . . . Finally, the polishing up can start, and the typing or re-write, as appropriate.

Discussion of the writing process often allows us to identify where we have particular problems . . .

Czerniewska (1992:84-85)

Concluding activity

Read aloud, or ask somebody else to read aloud, something that you have written. How does it sound? Does it flow well and make sense to the listener? Is it interesting? From doing this, and by considering feedback that you have been given, make a list of ways in which you can improve your writing.

Chapter 14
Observation in childcare and education

In this chapter we explore some ways in which observation is used to enhance children's care and education. Some methods of observation are discussed and exemplified as a basis for understanding the relationships between observations, assessment and planning in early childhood provision.

> ## Vignette 14.1
>
> *Kylie goes towards the balancing beams where some other children are waiting to walk along the beams. She waits her turn and then walks along the wide plank quite confidently from start to finish, placing one foot in front of the other and with her arms slightly extended to her sides. When she goes to the narrow beam she puts her hand out for the teacher to hold and steady her as she walks along the planks. She returns to the queue for the narrow beam a further three times, each time holding her hand out for the teacher to help her.*

Introduction

This opening observation, of a three-year-old-child who has recently started at nursery school, illustrates the type of information that may be recorded to support and promote care and learning in early years settings. From just this short observation, several of Kylie's achievements can be noted: her competence in walking along the wider balance beam unaided; her ability to seek the teacher's help to achieve the challenge of balancing along the narrow beam; her capacity to wait and take turns with other children; and her persistence in attempting the more difficult task.

The observation can be shared with Kylie's parents as part of discussions about how well she is settling into the nursery environment. It can also be discussed with colleagues, along with other observations, for considering Kylie's experiences and planning new opportunities and next steps for her learning. For example, the teacher may reflect that rather than holding Kylie's hand on all three attempts at the narrow balance beam she could have begun to encourage Kylie to try the task independently, with her hand there to be grasped, if needed.

These comments on one short vignette indicate the potential of observation as a tool for care and learning, when it is used in childcare practice. In this chapter some uses of observation for care and education are discussed and then some methods of observation used in early years settings are outlined.

Becoming observant

Our observations of other human beings are always central to care and caring relationships. When we are with family and close friends we notice and interpret their facial expressions, body language, tone of voice and other physical features to make inferences about the state of their well-being. Likewise, whenever we are with children and have professional responsibility for them we have to be watchful to ensure that we get to know them and respond to their needs through the cues we receive. By acquiring sound observation skills, practitioners can become observant and responsive to children (Luff 2010).

The care of babies and very young children requires observant practitioners who show sensitivity and respect and who understand and respond to their needs, and so build close and reciprocal relationships (Petrie and Owen 2005). The child who has experienced observant care will find it easier to become a sensitive observer and show empathy her/himself. Elfer (2005) recognises the challenges of close involvement with very young children, especially the emotional demands of containing their feelings, and recommends engaging with observation in ways that take into account how an observer feels when observing a child's experience. This can contribute to understanding, relating to, and caring for the child. For this practitioners are advised to 'observe more and do less' (Gerber 2002:63).

It is important that those who work in early years settings become empathic observant practitioners who are tuned into children. In Vignette 14.1 the teacher notices Kylie extend her hand for support and responds by holding her hand as she walks along the narrow beam. Reacting with support to cues from the child can be important for developing positive and trusting relationships. While being observant in this way can be an important way of listening to children, observant responses to children may also play a part in formal observation and record keeping.

Formal uses of observation

Sharing information

In addition to becoming an observant practitioner, there is also formal observing and recording that occurs as part of early years care practice. For example, day nursery staff, and some childminders, complete day sheets or diaries in which they record observations of daily routines to inform parents (Luff 2009). In some settings the day sheet or diary may include details of what the child has played with and perhaps even a digital photograph of them engaged in their favourite activity. This information is important when sharing care with parents. Early childhood care is not simply about the relationships between the child and the early years practitioner, but is usually a complex three-way triangle constructed between the parents, child and early years practitioner (Hohmann 2007). Observations can be a vital part of shared caring and decision making, in which children's daily experience is valued and negotiated.

It is acknowledged that these daily diaries have their own limitations as they record less than what is actually happening and certain forms of information are difficult to capture. Elfer (2005) notices that the ways in which practitioners speak about the children they work with are much richer and more informative than the observation records set down in writing.

Observation for planning and assessment

Observation is also used for planning for children's learning and assessing their progress. These observations enable practitioners to understand and appreciate children's interests and abilities in order to plan worthwhile, educative experiences to extend their learning. They also provide the evidence for assessing children's progress against, for instance, developmental milestones or statutory assessment frameworks (Black and William 1998; Drummond 1993). In this aspect, observation forms part of everyday practice, where practitioners attempt with anecdotal observations to capture evidence of children's achievements, and possible challenges as they occur.

In a busy setting, it is more likely that these observations will take place in an informal way. Practitioners record children's behaviours, achievements and difficulties, as they happen. These anecdotal observations collected over time build up a picture of a child's learning needs and attainments. For example, watching Kylie on the balance beams you might note down: *'Walked along the wide beam independently, using arms outstretched for balance'*; and/or *'Walked along narrow beam holding adult's hand'*. These could then be filed in Kylie's records.

You can either focus on a particular child or several children. As you are playing and interacting with the children, when you notice a child demonstrate a skill then you can jot down her/his name and what s/he has said or done and then add your initials and date it. These observations are filed in individual children's records. Examples of such recordings are shown:

Jake - Lined up the plastic mini-beasts in size order saying, 'Which one's the biggest? Which one's the next biggest?' (PL 27/01/2009)
Shakira - held scissors in right hand and snipped all round the edges of a card held in her left hand. (SA 3/06/2010)

The advantages of these anecdotal observations are that they do not take long to record and are part of everyday practice, not requiring regular time out to conduct them. Three common criticisms of this approach are: first, observations are often unsystematic and thus may be considered unreliable; second, while recording specific behaviours that they find interesting, observers may miss other notable achievements; and, third, if too much focus is placed upon behaviours that are linked with the curriculum goals children may become aware that certain behaviours are valued and others overlooked.

One way to counteract these criticisms is to plan a schedule of observations in order to focus on a certain number of children each day or week. For example in a nursery school, all staff record notes about three to four children each day and, at the end of the day, they use these recordings to reflect and discuss children's progress and plan for their learning. Filed observations are subsequently used as evidence to complete statutory assessment profiles (Papatheodorou 2010b). This system is used in the 'possible lines of direction' method of observation (discussed later in this chapter).

In general, observation for children's learning and assessment requires that practitioners adopt reflective and analytical approaches to gain a fuller understanding of children's learning or behaviour, plan for further learning opportunities, and assess their progress. The systematic handling of observation records is a requirement, irrespective of how it has been collected. Anecdotal observations alone do not constitute evidence. Worthington (2010) argues that observations must go beyond just seeing and noting what has occurred to explore the underlying meanings and support children's learning further. This thoughtful and carefully planned approach has been detailed in Vignettes 12.1 and 12.2, which dealt with issues of particular concern.

Observation for evaluation

Observational methods are often used to evaluate the learning environment and the quality and effectiveness of early years provision. The focus on the environment is important, as the places where care and education are offered are likely to shape the feelings, thoughts and behaviour of those who work and play there (Papatheodorou 2010c). Standardised rating scales such as the Early Childhood Environment Rating Scale (ECERS) and the later Infant/Toddler Environment Rating Scale (ITERS) are well-established tools of observational evaluation. First developed in the USA by Harms and Clifford (1980) and Harms et al. (1990; 2004) they are based on seven dimensions of quality (space and furnishings, personal care routines, language and reasoning, activities, interaction, programme structure and provision for parents and staff). For each of these dimensions, or sub-scales, there are different items that observers must score on a seven-point rating scale. Used in many parts of the world, they have been adapted for audit and self-improvement initiatives and research projects. The Effective Provision of Pre-school Education (EPPE) research team, for example, developed the ECERS-E by adding new sub-scales for literacy, mathematics, science and environment, and diversity (Sylva et al. 2003).

Another tool used in quality assurance and improvement, and research, is the Leuven Involvement Scale created by Laevers (1994) to judge children's responses to their experiences in early years settings. The scale provides a tool with which to rate children's involvement, from no involvement or activity (which scores zero) to sustained, intense involvement (which scores five). Children's involvement is judged by observing signals related to the child's body language, for example concentration, posture, creative response, energy and persistence.

The Leuven Scale was used in the Effective Early Learning project as a basis for quality improvement in early childhood settings (Pascal et al. 1994; Pascal and Bertram 1997). On the basis of the scores, staff drew up plans to improve provision in order to provide children with more opportunities to become deeply involved in learning. Once the improvements were implemented, the settings repeated the observations of involvement in order to see whether children had become more involved in activities.

It is possible for informal audit tools to be devised by students or practitioners. These can be thoughtful and rigorous if they are based on conceptions of quality from literature and research as well as practitioners' own beliefs and experience about what is valuable in a setting. For example, a student having read about creativity in the early years might draw up observation schedules to look at opportunities for creativity within a setting and children's creative responses. Such observation schedules, which are likely to be context specific, will have validity within a particular setting but cannot claim the wider reliability of standardised tools.

Other approaches to observation

Three other methods of using observation to understand and then promote children's learning are outlined below, providing enough detail for readers to try them out in early years settings. These are: possible lines of direction, learning stories and pedagogical documentation.

Possible lines of direction

In this method of observation everything that is seen during a ten-minute observation is noted as a narrative account. Educators who use this method often choose a few children each week to focus upon and record three narrative observations of each child, for about ten minutes, at different times of the day, in order to identify *possible lines of direction* and use these for planning (Whalley 2001). The observation of Kylie, in Vignette 14.1, would be an example of an extract from this type of narrative observation. Video evidence might also be used for this type of observation.

The emphasis of possible lines of direction is on using insights from the observations to understand the child's current interests and to use these insights to provide more activities to support their learning. The observations are discussed among the staff team and also with parents. This enables the observer to see patterns in the child's behaviour and identify key interests. More opportunities can be given for the child to practise developing skills and use them for sharing information with parents.

Disadvantages of this method include the time that it takes to record and discuss the observations and the emphasis on just a few children each week when creating short-term curriculum plans. Advocates of the approach would point out the value of spending time in this activity, particularly having in-depth discussions about each child based on evidence that parents will value. The criticism that planning might then focus on an individual is countered by a view that children of a similar age are likely to have similar priorities in their learning and thus an activity designed with a particular child in mind is likely to be engaging for others within a class or group (Whalley 2001; Athey 1991).

Learning stories

Planning with a focus on extending a child's learning is also a feature of the *learning stories* approach to recording children's educational experiences, pioneered in New Zealand (Podmore 2006; Carr 2001). Learning stories were developed as narrative assessments linked with the principles and strands of the bi-cultural 'Te Whāriki' early childhood curriculum in New Zealand (Carr 2001). A basic learning story format provides space for recording narrative observations of the child's learning, usually celebrating a positive achievement that provides evidence of the learning dispositions valued in the five strands of Te Whāriki (belonging, well-being, exploration, communication and contribution). Children collaborate in the creation of their learning stories,

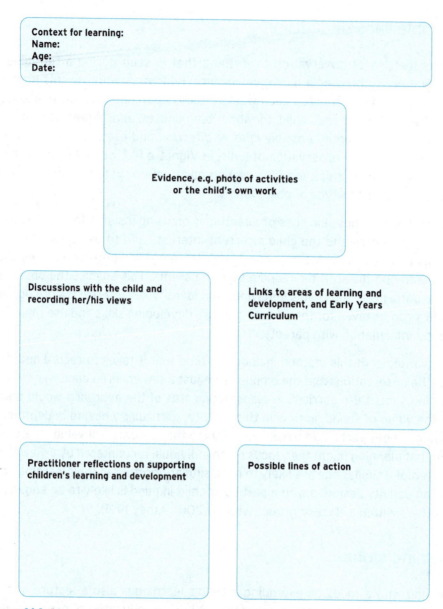

Context for learning:
Name:
Age:
Date:

**Evidence, e.g. photo of activities
or the child's own work**

**Discussions with the child and
recording her/his views**

**Links to areas of learning and
development, and Early Years
Curriculum**

**Practitioner reflections on supporting
children's learning and development**

Possible lines of action

Figure 14.1 Sample of a Learning Journey form (adapted from DCSF, n.d)

sometimes the description of the learning is narrated by the child, and parents also have a voice.

Documenting learning stories places value on what has been observed and allows for a review of what has been achieved and shared planning of future opportunities for learning. Spaces for a short analysis of the learning and a plan for what could come next are included as part of the learning story record (see Figure 14.1). Children's learning stories, often illustrated with drawings and photographs, are combined in a portfolio. As the emphasis is upon the child as a competent learner and the child and family have participated in the telling of the stories, the portfolio can be a source of pride in each child's achievements. When the child moves on from kindergarten to school, it can provide rich evidence of their learning and a basis to get to know the child and build a relationship with her/him (Peters 2009).

Pedagogical documentation

Dahlberg et al. (2007) suggest that the term 'observation' implies that the adult observer is making assessments of a child, largely based on developmental norms, with an assumption that factual information about the child can be accurately recorded. They argue that, as seen in the pre-schools of Reggio Emilia (Rinaldi 2005, 2006; Edwards et al. 1998) pedagogical documentation can be seen as a more open and interactive approach to representing and making sense of children's learning.

Creating pedagogical documentation involves collecting and displaying evidence of children's learning. In Reggio Emilia, this often focuses upon *progettazione* – shared, open-ended project work arising from children's interests and following their investigations. The role of the observant adult is to take notes and photographs, make audio- and video-recordings and collect examples of the children's work in progress, such as drawings or models. The educator has to be an active listener at all times, making sense of what children are saying, supporting them in expressing their thinking and displaying this as a key part of the documentation. The documentation then serves three purposes. It offers the children a way of reflecting on and revisiting their learning in order to make further progress. It displays the learning process to others, thus involving the broader school community and including parents. Most importantly, it forms a basis for the teachers' in-depth analyses of the children's learning and consequent decision making about the resources, techniques and suggestions to be offered to the children in order to support their meaning making.

This approach has been adapted for use in Swedish pre-schools where the same approach is taken to documenting and using evidence to foster children's learning (Dahlberg et al. 2007). It is more difficult to implement in an English context, as the curriculum is more prescribed and early years educators rarely have the time to prepare the documentation well and reflect upon it thoroughly. There are, nevertheless, examples of adults presenting accounts of children's work in ways that enable them to revisit meaningful projects and celebrate significant learning (DfES 2006; Beels 2004).

Summary

This chapter has shown the significance of observation for enhancing children's care and education. Discussion has focused on ways in which observation can be used to improve care for the youngest children and develop meaningful opportunities for children's learning. The importance of observation as part of a commitment to understand and promote children's learning has been empha-sised and exemplified through accounts of three approaches to observation (possible lines of direction, learning stories, and pedagogical documentation), all of which are linked to assessment and planning for learning within early childhood education.

Concluding activity

Review the methods of observation used in an early years setting. This could be the place where you work or somewhere you have visited for your observa-tions. How are observations used to support and promote children's care and education?

Chapter 15
Conclusion – the power of observation

In this concluding chapter we provide an overview of the skills and knowledge required for sound observations. We outline some of the challenges observers experience and highlight the importance of self-awareness in understanding observations. We consider observation as a powerful cultural tool for learning about children and professional practice as well as for understanding our own learning.

> ## Vignette 15.1
>
> Through completing these observations, I have been able to learn the skills necessary for child observation, revise my knowledge of child development, refine my ability to apply theory to practice, learn about the relationship between play and learning and the implications of such knowledge for early years practitioners. Although I tried to remain totally objective throughout all the observations I cannot say that my personal opinions and beliefs did not affect my interpretation of the observed behaviours; also my presence may have affected the way the observed child behaved.
>
> *Excerpt from a student's writing*

> ## Vignette 15.2
>
> In my capacity as an observer, I have always tried to give a valid, true representation of the child's behaviour or actions. I have sought, whenever possible, to ratify my observations by cross-referencing them with others. With time I came to realise the value of hindsight; of reflecting upon, analysing and interpreting the data; and the need for sharing one's thoughts and evaluations with colleagues and carers. Carrying out observations is not simply a note-taking exercise, but rather an informed and reflective appraisal of one's own practice. There are no prescriptive formulas for carrying out observations; what emanates, in terms of one's conduct, approach, recording and reflection, is highly personal and individual.
>
> *Excerpt from a student's writing*

Introduction

The two vignettes above are excerpts from students' writing that focused on what and how they had learned through observation. In Vignette 15.1 the observer outlined her/his learning about observational skills, the child and relevant practice, and being a thoughtful and reflective learner. In Vignette 15.2 the observer detailed elements of observation that s/he found significant. S/he also acknowledged observation as a complex and sometimes ambiguous process that requires the observer to be acutely self-aware.

The value of observation, as acknowledged in the first vignette, is well established and, indeed, students are taught observational skills and encouraged to apply them to learn about children and practice. How we learn and what we learn about ourselves as learners, as illustrated in the second vignette, is less explicitly addressed. In this book we have sought to redress the balance by advocating a systematic and rigorous observational process for students both to acquire relevant observational skills and apply them, and, by doing so, to become aware of their own learning, that is, to see their learning beyond skill acquisition, but requiring engagement and self-appraisal.

In this chapter we revisit and discuss some of the inherent challenges of observation and the opportunities it offers as a learning tool.

Overview of the observational process

Child observation as an empirical tool requires that learners are aware of available methods of observation, acquire appropriate skills and competencies related to planning observations and ethical issues, and an appreciation of the role of personal attitudes and the observer stance. Such issues become significant in doing and recording observations and form the basis for initial reflections. While reflection on observations provides initial ideas and insights about the observed child and her/his context, it is the systematic analysis and interrogation that lead to well-substantiated conclusions and ideas. These processes are as important in learning as in doing research and informing practice.

Challenges of observation

Learning these skills is not without challenges. This is illustrated by the feedback from a group of our students who were asked to reflect upon their observations. They identified a wide range of challenges that refer to the three interacting entities of the observational process, that is: the *observed child*, the *setting* and the *observer*. Those related to the *observed child* included: the child recognises you as a playmate; seeks your help or wants your attention; the child is exceedingly talkative, friendly, questioning or interrupting; the child feels unwell; the child is moody or upset.

Setting-related challenges included: adults act differently because of the observer's presence (observer effect); adults focus on the observed child especially in group situations; adults interact with the observer and want to know their opinions; unanticipated programme changes that compromise the intended focus of the observation; safety issues; discomfort and/or distracting noises from children's play or from outside.

The majority of the challenges were related to the *observer*. These included:

- Sources of bias that threaten objectivity, such as knowing the child well and finding it hard to be objective; being strongly influenced by what other people say about the child.

- Observation experience triggers repressed memories; over-identification with the child; finding it difficult to concentrate for a sustained period of time.

- Preoccupation with own worries; overwhelmed by own emotions; pressure of time; lack of sustained commitment; disruption to the observation arrangements.

- Insecure and awkward feelings for a variety of reasons, such as not knowing people very well; having anxieties about 'putting upon' parents or early years professionals or feeling obliged to help.

- Wider professional issues such as maintaining confidentiality; staff and parents wanting to see or have copies of observations; concerns about other people's handling of children; and about the quality of provision for children.

These challenges potentially disrupt, distract and/or block the observational process and as such they need to be dealt with. Therefore, as an observer you will need to explicitly identify your challenges and acknowledge your responses and actions. Some responses and actions may be immediate and instantaneous, as a result of *reflection in action*. Others may be delayed, requiring thoughtful *reflection on action*. Reflecting on your challenges, responses and actions you will gradually develop heightened self-awareness of your skills and knowledge as well as your own attitudes and values.

Personal experience that exposes doubts and ambiguity in our thinking and leaves us in a state of perplexity, dissonance and incongruity often leads us to search for solutions that shed light on our held beliefs or views (Dewey 1991). For example, the student's entry about methodology in her learning journal (quoted in Chapter 13) shows how an observer dealt with the challenge regarding her observer stance, by providing a rationale that reflects her own values and attitudes.

Observation and self-awareness

These challenges demonstrate that observation is not just an accumulation of skills and competencies. It is a process that requires heightened self-awareness as well as awareness of the observed and the setting. By being in a state of constant alertness to notice and weigh contextual challenges and by becoming aware of her/his own responses, the observer will be enabled to deal with ambiguities and uncertainties, and address dilemmas created throughout observations. As the observer in Vignette 15.2 has acknowledged, there are no recipes to follow when doing observation. Instead this process is highly personal and individual, dependent on one's conduct, reflective appraisal and appreciation of hindsight. Ultimately, these personal qualities impact on observations, but they are also further developed by following a thorough and reflective observational process.

There are however additional layers of meaning explored through collective reflection and systematic analysis and interrogation. Collective reflection allows personal values and attitudes to be subjected to scepticism and critique by others (e.g. peers, tutors, professionals or parents). Systematic analysis and interrogation also enables the observer to consider her/his observation in the light of extant knowledge because, as Dewey (1991) has argued, the mind must be in possession of some knowledge to make thinking possible. Through negotiating and weighing these processes the observer aims to derive meaning that has collective currency among peers and/or practitioners and, if appropriate, to inform and guide action.

The power of observation

Child observation is a powerful cultural tool that offers learners first-hand experience to learn about children and professional practice and to make sense of their own learning (Kolb 1984). It leads to learners' acculturation by introducing them to ways of thinking and doing things in a particular discipline or profession. It allows them to work alongside knowledgeable others and be facilitated by them to reach new meanings and practices, which, in turn, may also impact on that culture (Wells 1999). It also offers transferable skills for learning.

Child observation as a tool for learning requires background knowledge of the discipline and professional practice under study, appropriate skills and heightened self-awareness. It demands an ability and willingness to reflect

and interrogate personal and professional beliefs and attitudes, and to subject them to critiques by others and to consider their perspectives. It requires
careful weighing of evidence and explicit acknowledgement of personal values.
Learning is as much an emotional affair as it is a cognitive process. This makes
learning through observation an exciting and revealing journey. The tutors support, facilitate, challenge and stretch students' learning, and personal and professional development, and through this process the tutors learn themselves. It
is in this spirit that we have written this book.

References, Appendices and Index

References

Adler P.A. and Adler P. (1987) *Membership Roles in Field Research*, Newbury Park, CA: Sage

Alderson, P. (2004) Ethics, in S. Fraser, V. Lewis, S. Ding, M. Kellett and C. Robinson (eds), *Doing Research with Children and Young People*, London: Sage Publications in association with Open University Press

Alexander, E. (2002) Childcare students: learning or imitating?, *Forum*, 44 (1): 24-26

Allport, G.W. (1973) Attitudes in the history of social psychology, in N. Warren and M. Jahoda (eds), *Attitudes*, Harmondsworth: Penguin Books

Angrosino, M.V. and Mays de Pérez , K.A (2003) Rethinking observation: from method to context, in N.K. Denzin and Y.S. Lincoln (eds), *Collecting and Interpreting Qualitative Materials*, Thousand Oaks, CA: Sage

Arnold, C. (1999) *Child Development and Learning 2-5 Years: Georgia's Story*, London: Paul Chapman

Arnold, C. (2003) *Observing Harry: Child Development and Learning 0-5*, Maidenhead: Open University Press

Ash, S. (1952) *Social Psychology*, Englewood Cliffs, NJ: Prentice-Hall

Athey, C. (1991) *Extending Thought in Young Children*, London: Paul Chapman

Atkinson (1989) Goffman's poetics, *Human Studies*, 12: 59-76

Auerbach, C.F. and Silverstein, L. (2003) *Qualitative Data: An Introduction to Coding and Analysis*, New York: New York University Press

Bandura, A. (1977) *Social Learning Theory*, Englewoods Cliffs, NJ: Prentice-Hall

Bandura, A. (1986) *Social Foundations of Thought and Action: A Social-cognitive Theory*, Englewoods Cliffs, NJ: Prentice-Hall

Bartholomew, L. and Bruce, T. (1993) *Getting to Know You: A Guide to Record Keeping in Early Childhood Education and Care*, London: Hodder & Stoughton

Bassey, M. (1999) *Case Study Research in Educational Settings*, Maidenhead: Open University Press

Beels, P. (2004) All about documentation, *Nursery World*, 5 February [online] available at: http://www.nurseryworld.co.uk/news/713096/share-documentation/ [accessed 3 January 2009]

Bell, L. and Nutt, L. (2003) Divided loyalties, divided expectations: research ethics, professional and occupational responsibilities, in M. Mauther, M. Birch, J. Jessop and T. Miller (eds), *Ethics in Qualitative Research*, London: Sage

BERA (2004) *Revised Ethical Guidelines for Educational Research*, Southwell: BERA

Bissex, G. (1980) *Gyns at Wrk*, Cambridge, MA: Harvard University Press

Black, P. and Wiliam, D. (1998) Inside the black box: raising standards through classroom assessment, *Phi Delta Kappa*, 80 (2): 139-44

Breen, L.J. (2007) The researcher 'in the middle': negotiating the insider/outsider dichotomy, *The Australian Community Psychologist*, 9 (1): 163-74

Broadhead, P. (2006) Developing an understanding of young children's learning through play: the place of observation, interaction and reflection, *British Educational Research Journal*, 32 (2): 191–207

Bronfenbrenner, U. (1979) *The Ecology of Human Development*, Cambridge, MA: Harvard University Press

Brookfield, S.D. (1995) *Becoming a Critically Reflective Teacher*, San Francisco, CA: Jossey-Bass

Bruce, T. (1991) *Time to Play in Early Childhood Education*, London: Hodder & Stoughton

Bruner, J.S. (1990) *Acts of Meaning*, Cambridge, MA: Harvard University Press

Bruner, J.S. and Tagiuri, R. (1954) The perception of people, in G. Lindzey (ed.), *Handbook of Social Psychology*, Reading, MA: Addison-Wesley (vol. 2)

Bruyn, S. (1966) *The Human Perspective in Sociology: The Methodology of Participant Observation*, Englewood Cliffs, NJ: Prentice-Hall

Calhoun, J.F. and Acocella, J.R. (1990) *Psychology of Adjustment and Human Relationships* (3rd edn), New York: McGraw-Hill

Carr, M. (2001) *Assessment in Early Childhood Settings: Learning Stories*, London: Paul Chapman

Charmaz, K. (2006) *Constructing Grounded Theory: A Practical Guide Through Qualitative Analysis*, London: Sage

Coady, M.M. (2001) Ethics in early childhood research, in G. MacNaughton, S.A. Rolfe and I. Siraj-Blatchford (eds), *Doing Early Childhood Research: International Perspectives on Theory and Practice*, Buckingham: Open University Press

Cohen, D.H., Stern, V. and Balaban, N. (1997) *Observing and Recording the Behavior of Young Children* (4th edn), New York: Teachers College Press

Cook, M. (1979) *Perceiving Others: The Psychological Interpersonal Perception*, London: Methuen

Corsaro, W.A. (1985) *Friendship and Peer Culture in the Early Years*, Norwood, NJ: Ablex

Corsaro, W.A. (2003) *"We're Friends, Right?" Inside Kid's Culture*, Washington, DC: Joseph Henry Press

Coulon, A. (1995) *Ethnomethodology*, Thousand Oaks, CA: Sage

Creswell, J.W. (2007) *Qualitative Inquiry and Research Design: Choosing Among Five Approaches* (2nd edn), Thousand Oaks, CA: Sage

Czerniewska, P. (1992) *Learning about Writing*, Oxford: Blackwell

DCSF (nd) Early Years Foundation Stage: Template for Learning Journeys, available online at: http://nationalstrategies.standards.dcsf.gov.uk/node/84404 (accessed 4 May 2011)

Dahlberg, G., Moss, P. and Pence, A. (1999) *Beyond Quality in Early Childhood Education: Postmodern Perspective*, London: Falmer Press

Dahlberg, G., Moss, P. and Pence, A. (2007) *Beyond Quality in Early Childhood Education: Languages of Evaluation*, London: Routledge

Daniels, H. (2005) *An Introduction to Vygotsky* (2nd edn), London: Routledge

Darwin, C. (1877) A biographical sketch of an infant, *Mind, A Quarterly Review of Psychology and Philosophy*, 2 (7): 285–94 [online] available at: http://darwin-online.org.uk/content/frameset?itemID=F1877_infant_F1779&viewtype=textpageseq=1 [accessed 12 December 2009]

Darwin, C. (2006) *On the Origins of Species by Means of Natural Selection or the Preservation of Favoured Races in the Struggle for Life*, Mineola, NY: Dover Publications [originally published by John Marry, London, 1859]

Delamont, S. (2002) *Fieldwork in Educational Settings: Methods, Pitfalls and Perspectives* (2nd edn), London and New York: Routledge

Denzin, N.K. and Lincoln, Y.S. (2000) *Handbook of Qualitative Research* (2nd edn), London: Sage.

Denzin, N.K. and Lincoln, Y.S. (2003) *Collecting and Interpreting Qualitative Materials* (2nd edn), Thousand Oaks, CA: Sage

Dewey, J. (1991) *How We Think*, New York: Prometheus Books [originally published by D.C. Heath, Lexington, MA, 1910]

Dewey, J. (1997a) *Experience and Education*, New York: Touchstone [originally published by Kappa Delta Pi, 1938]

Dewey (1997b) *Democracy and Education, Introduction to Philosophy of Education*, New York: Simon & Schuster [originally published by The Macmillan Company, 1916]

Dey, I. (1993) *Qualitative Data Analysis*, London: Routledge

DfES (2006) Celebrating Young Children (poster and DVD pack). London: DfES Publications

Donaldson, M. (1978) *Children's Minds*, London: Fontana

Drummond, M.J. (1993) *Assessing Children's Learning*, London: David Fulton

Drummond, M.J. (1998) Observing children, in S. Smidt (ed.), *The Early Years: A Reader*, London: Routledge

Edwards, A. (2001) Qualitative designs and analysis, in G. MacNaughton, S.A. Rolfe and I. Siraj-Blatchford (eds), *Doing Early Childhood Research*, Maidenhead: Open University Press

Edwards, C.P., Gandini, L. and Forman, G.E. (1998) *The Hundred Languages of Children: The Reggio Emilia Approach – Advanced Reflections* (2nd edn), Westport, CT: Ablex Publishing Corporation

Eiser, J.R. (1990) *Social Judgement,* Milton Keynes: Open University Press

Elfer, P. (2005) Observation matters, in L. Abbott and A. Langston (eds), *Birth to Three Matters,* Maidenhead: Open University Press

Ely, M., Vinz, R., Downing, M. and Anzul, M. (1997) *On Writing Qualitative Research: Living by Words*, London: Falmer Press

ESRC (2010) *Research Ethics Framework* [online] available at: http://www. esrcsocietytoday.ac.uk/ESRCInfoCentre/Images/Framework%20for% 20Research%20Ethics%202010_tcm6-35811.pdf [accessed 14 October 2010]

Fawcett, M. (1996) *Learning Through Child Observation*, London: Jessica Kingsley

Fawcett, M. (2009) *Learning Through Child Observation* (2nd edn), London: Jessica Kingsley

Festinger, L. (1957) *A Theory of Cognitive Dissonance*, Stanford, CA: Stanford University Press

Fetterman, D.M. (1998) *Ethnography Step by Step,* Thousand Oaks, CA: Sage

Freud, S. (1960) *The Ego and the Id* [standard edn with biographical introduction by Peter Gray], New York and London: W.W. Norton

Gall, M.D., Gall, J.P. and Borg, W.R. (2010) *Applying Educational Research* (6th edn), Boston, MA: Pearson

Gerber, M. (2002) *Caring for Children with Respect* (2nd edn), Los Angeles, CA: Resources for Infant Educarers

Gesell, A. (1950) *The First Five Years of Life*, London: Methuen

Gibbs, G. (1988) *Learning by Doing: A Guide to Teaching and Learning Methods*, Oxford: Further Education Unit, Oxford Brookes University

Gillen, J. and Hall, N. (2001) 'Hiya, Mum!' An analysis of pretence telephone play in a nursery setting, *Early Years*, 21 (1): 15-24

Gillett, A., Hammond, A. and Martala, M. (2009) *Successful Academic Writing*, Harlow: Pearson

Gold, R.L. (1958) Roles in sociological field observation, *Social Forces*, 36: 217-33

Greig, A., Taylor, J. and MacKay, T. (2007) *Doing Research with Children* (2nd edn), London: Sage

Hall, G.S. (1893) *The Contents of Children's Minds on Entering School*, New York and Chicago, IL: E.L. Kellogg

Hall, G.S. (1897a) A study of fears, *American Journal of Psychology*, 8: 147-249

Hall, G.S. (1897b) *The Story of a Sand Pile*, New York and Chicago, IL: E.L. Kellogg

Harding, J. and Meldon-Smith, L. (1996) *How to Make Observations and Assessments*, London: Hodder & Stoughton

Harding, J. and Meldon-Smith, L. (2002) *How to Make Observations and Assessment* (2nd edn), Abingdon: Hodder & Stoughton

Hargreaves, D.H. (2004) *Learning for Life: The Foundations for Lifelong Learning*, Bristol: The Policy Press

Hargreaves, L. (2002) Seeing clearly: observation in the primary classroom, in J. Moyles and G. Robinson (eds), *Beginning Teaching, Beginning Learning in Primary Education* (2nd edn), Buckingham: Open University Press

Harms, T. and Clifford, R.M. (1980) *Early Childhood Rating Scale*, New York: Teachers College Press

Harms, T., Clifford, R.M. and Cryer, D. (2004) *Early Childhood Rating Scale* (rev. edn), New York: Teachers College Press

Harms, T., Cryer, D. and Clifford, R.M. (1990) *Infant/Toddler Rating Scale*, New York: Teachers College Press

Hastrup, K. (1995) *A Passage to Anthropology: Between Experience and Theory*, London: Routledge

Heider, F. (1958) *The Psychology of Interpersonal Relations*, New York: J. Wiley & Sons

Hein, G.E. (1991) *Constructivist Learning Theory*, The Museum and the Needs of People CECA (International Committee of Museum Educators) Conference, Jerusalem Israel, 15-22 October, [online] available at: http://www.exploratorium.edu/IFI/resources/constructivistlearning.html [accessed 4 October 2010]

Hobart, C. and Frankel, J. (2004) *A Practical Guide to Child Observation and Assessment*, (3rd edn), Cheltenham: Nelson Thornes

Hohmann, U. (2007) Rights, expertise and negotiations in care and education, *Early Years*, 27 (1): 33-46

Isaacs, S. (1929) *The Nursery Years*, London: Routledge & Kegan Paul

Isaacs, S. (1930) *Intellectual Growth in Young Children*, London: Routledge & Kegan Paul

Isaacs, S. (1948) *Childhood and After: Some Essays and Clinical Studies*, London: Routledge

Jorgensen, D.L. (1989) *Participant Observation: A Methodology of Human Studies* (Applied Social Research Methods, vol. 15), Thousand Oaks, CA: Sage

Kail, R.V. (2004) *Children and their Development* (3rd edn), Upper Saddle River, NJ: Pearson Prentice-Hall

Kalantzis, M. and Cope, B. (2008) *New Learning: Elements of a Science of Education*, Cambridge: Cambridge University Press

Knott, K. (2005) Insider/outsider perspectives, in J.R. Hinnells (ed.), *The Routledge Companion of Religion*, London: Routledge

Kolb, D.A. (1984) *Experiential Learning: Experience as a Source of Learning and Development*, Englewood Cliffs, NJ: Prentice-Hall

Kozulin, A., Gindis, B., Ageyev, V.S. and Miller, S.M. (2003) Introduction: socio-cultural theory and education – students, teachers and knowledge, in A. Kozulin, B. Gindis, V.S. Ageyev and S.M. Miller (eds), *Vygotsky's Educational Theory in Cultural Context*, Cambridge, Cambridge University Press

Laishley, J. (1987) *Working with Young Children: Encouraging their Development and Dealing with Problems* (2nd edn), London: Hodder Arnold HSS

Laevers, F. (1994) *The Leuven Involvement Scale for Young Children LIS-YC Manual (Experiential Education Series 1)*, Leuven: Centre for Experiential Education

Lave, J. and Wenger, E. (1991) *Situated Learning: Legitimate Peripheral Participation*, Cambridge: Cambridge University Press

Leyens, J.P. and Codol, J.P. (1988) Social cognition, in M. Hewstone, W. Stroebe, J.P. Codol and G.M. Stephenson (eds), *Introduction to Social Psychology*, Oxford, Basil Blackwell

Luff, P. (2009) Observation for relational pedagogy, in T. Papatheodorou and J. Moyles (eds), *Learning Together in the Early Years: Exploring Relational Pedagogy*, London and New York: Routledge

Luff. P. (2010) Ways of seeing and knowing children: a case study of early years practitioners' understandings and uses of child observation during their first year of employment, Chelmsford: Anglia Ruskin University (unpublished PhD thesis)

MacNaughton, G. (2003) *Shaping Early Childhood*, Maidenhead: Open University Press

Mayall, B. (2000) Conversations with children: working with generational issues, in P. Christensen and A. James (eds), *Research with Children*, London: Routledge Falmer

McCormick, R. and Paechter, C. (1999) Introduction: learning and knowledge construction, in R. McCormick and C. Paechter (eds), *Learning and Knowledge*, London: Paul Chapman in association with Open University

Miller, L., Rustin, M., Rustin, M. and Shuttleworth, J. (1989) *Closely Observed Infants*, London: Duckworth

Montessori, M. (1912) *The Montessori Method: Scientific Pedagogy as Applied to Child Education in 'The Children's Houses' with Additions and Revisions by the Author*, trans. Anne E. George, New York: Frederick A. Stokes [online] available at: (http://digital.library.upenn.edu/women/montessori/method/method.html [accessed 14 November 2010]

Montessori, M. (1967) *The Absorbent Mind*, New York: Henry Holt

Moriarty, V. (1998) *Margaret McMillan: 'I learn, to succour the helpless'*, Nottingham: Educational Heretics Press

Morrow, V. (2005) Ethical issues in collaborative research with children, in A. Farrell (ed.), *Ethical Research with Children*, Maidenhead: Open University Press

Moyles, J., Adams, S. and Musgrove, A. (2002) *Study of Pedagogical Effectiveness in Early Learning (SPEEL)*, London: DfES

Mukherji, P. and O'Dea, T. (2000) *Understanding Children's Language and Literacy*, Cheltenham: Stanley Thornes

Murray, R. and Moore, S. (2006) *Handbook of Academic Writing*, Maidenhead: Open University Press.

NAEYC (2005) *Code of Ethical Conduct and Statement of Commitment, Position Statement* (revised April 2005) [online] available at: http://www.naeyc.org/files/naeyc/file/positions/PSETH05.pdf [accessed 14 October 2010]

Nutbrown, C. (1996) *Respectful Educators - Capable Learners: Children's Rights and Early Education*, London: Paul Chapman

Osgood, C.E. and Tannenbaum, P.H. (1955) The principle of congruity in the prediction of attitude change, *Psychological Review*, 62: 42-55

Paley, V.G. (1981) *Wally's Stories: Conversations in Kindergarten*, Cambridge, MA: Harvard University Press

Paley, V.G. (1986) *Boys and Girls: Superheroes in the Doll Corner*, Chicago, IL: Chicago University Press

Paley, V.G. (1988) *Mollie is Three: Growing Up in School*, Chicago, IL: Chicago University Press

Paley, V.G. (1990) *The Boy Who Would Be A Helicopter*, Cambridge, MA: Harvard University Press

Papatheodorou, T. (2005) *Behaviour Problems in the Early Years: A Guide for Understanding and Support*, London: Routledge

Papatheodorou, T. (2010a) *Sensory Play, Pilot Research Project*, funded by an EEDA Innovation Voucher: 09/062, report submitted to Play to Z, Chelmsford: Anglia Ruskin University

Papatheodorou, T. (2010b) Understanding young children's behaviour, research project (in progress)

Papatheodorou, T. (2010c) The pedagogy of play(ful) learning environments, in J. Moyles (ed.), *Thinking about Play: Developing a Reflective Approach*, Maidenhead: McGraw Hill/Open University Press

Pascal, C. and Bertram, A.D. (1997) *Effective Early Learning: Case Studies of Improvement*, London: Hodder & Stoughton.

Pascal, C., Bertram, A.D. and Ramsden, F. (1994) *Effective Early Learning: The Quality Evaluation and Development Process*, Worcester: Amber

Pennington, D.C. (1986) *Essential Social Psychology*, London: Arnold/Hodder & Stoughton

Peters, S. (2009) Responsive reciprocal relationships: the heart of the Te Whākiri curriculum, in T. Papatheodorou and J. Moyles (eds), *Learning Together in the Early Years: Relational Pedagogy*, London: Routledge

Petrie, S. and Owen, S. (2005) *Authentic Relationships in Group Care for Infants and Toddlers: Resources for Infant Educarers (RIE) Principles into Practice*, London and Philadelphia: Jessica Kingsley

Piaget, J. (1926) *The Language and Thought of the Child* (trans. C. Cattegno and F.M. Hodgson), London: Routledge & Kegan Paul [first published by William Heinemann, London]

Piaget, J. (1951) *Play, Dreams and Imitation in Childhood* (English translation), London: Routledge & Kegan Paul.

Piaget, J. (1953) *The Origin of Intelligence in the Child* (English translation), London: Routledge & Kegan Paul.

Piaget, J. (2001) *The Psychology of Intelligence* (trans. M. Piercy and D.E. Berlyne), London: Routledge [first English edition published by Routledge & Kegan Paul, London 1950]

Piaget, J. (2002) *The Language and Thought of the Child* (3rd edn) (trans. Marjorie and Ruth Gabain), Abingdon: Routledge [first published by Paul Kegan, Trench & Co, London, 1926]

Piaget, J. and Inhelder, B. (1973) *Memory and Intelligence*, trans. A.J. Pomerans, New York: Basic Books

Piontelli, A. (1986) *Backwards in Time: A Study in Infant Observation by the Methods of Esther Bick*, Perthshire: Clunie Press

Piontelli, A. (2002) *Twins: From Fetus to Child*, London: Routledge

Podmore, V.N. (2006) *Observation: Origins and Approaches to Early Childhood Research and Practice*, Wellington: New Zealand Council for Educational Research

Raban, B., Ure, C. and Waniganayake, M. (2003) Multiple perspectives: acknowledging the virtue of complexity in measuring quality, *Early Years*, 23 (1): 67-77

Reed, J. (2007) *Appreciative Inquiry: Research for Change*, London: Sage

Reid, S. (1997) Introduction: psychoanalytic infant observation, in S. Reid (ed.), *Developments in Infant Observation: The Tavistock Model*, London: Routledge

Richards, L. (2005) *Handling Qualitative Data: A Practical Guide*, London: Sage

Rinaldi, C. (2005) Documentation and assessment: what is the relationship?, in A. Clark, A.T. Kjørholt and P. Moss (eds), *Beyond Listening*, Bristol: Policy Press

Rinaldi, C. (2006) *In Dialogue with Reggio Emilia: Listening, Researching and Learning*, London: RoutledgeFalmer

Roberts-Holmes, G. (2005) *Doing Your Early Years Project: A Step by Step Guide*, London: Paul Chapman

Roethlisberger, F.J. and Dickson, W.J. (1939) in *Management and the Worker: An Account of a Research Program Conducted by the Western Electric Company, Hawthorne Works, Chicago*, Cambridge MA: Harvard University Press

Rolfe, S.A. (2001) Direct observation, in G. MacNaughton, S.A. Rolfe and I. Siraj-Blatchford (eds), *Doing Early Childhood Research*, Maidenhead: Open University Press

Rustin, M. (2002) Looking in the Right Place: Complexity theory, psychoanalysis and infant observation, in A. Briggs (ed.), *Surviving Space: Papers on Infant Observation*, London: Karnac

Sarantakos, S. (1998) *Social Research* (2nd edn), Houndsmills, Basingstoke and London: Macmillan

Schön, D. (1983) *The Reflective Practitioner: How Professionals Think in Action*, London: Temple Smith

Sharman, C., Cross, W. and Vennis, D. (2004) *Observing Children: A Practical Guide* (2nd edn), London: Cassell

Shaver, K.G. (1987) *Principles of Social Psychology*, Hillsdale, NJ: Lawrence Erlbaum Associates

Sherif, M. and Hovland, G.I. (1961) *Social Judgment*, New Haven, CT: Yale University Press

Skinner, B.F. (1953) *Science and Human Behavior*, New York: Macmillan

Skinner, B.F. (1976) *About Behaviorism*, New York: Vintage Edition Books [originally published by Alfred A. Knopf, New York, 1974]

Sommer, R. and Sommer, B.B. (1986) *A Practical Guide to Behavioral Research: Tools and Techniques* (2nd edn), New York: Oxford University Press

Spradley, J.P. (1980) *Participant Observation*, New York: Holt, Rhinehart & Winston

Stahlberg, D. and Frey, D. (1988) Attitudes: structure, measurement and functions, in M. Hewstone, W. Stroebe, J. Codol and G.M. Stephenson (eds), *Introduction to Social Psychology*, Oxford: Basil Blackwell

Stake, R.E. (1995) *The Art of Case Study Research*, Thousand Oaks, CA and London: Sage

Stangor, C. (1988) Stereotype accessibility and information processing, *Personality and Social Psychology Bulletin*, 14: 694-708

Stangor, C. and Rumble, D.N. (1989) Strength of expectations and memory for social information: what we learn depends on how much we know, *Journal of Experimental Social Psychology*, 25: 18-36

Sternberg, J. (2005) *Infant Observation at the Heart of Training*, London: Karnac

Sylva, K., Siraj-Blatchford, I. and Taggart, B. (2003) *Assessing Quality in the Early Years: Early Childhood Environmental Rating Scale - Extension (ECERS-E) Four Curricula Subscales*, Stoke on Trent: Trentham Books

Tagiuri, R. (1969) Person perception, in G. Lindzey and E. Aronson (eds), *The Handbook of Social Psychology*, Reading, MA: Addison-Wesley (vol. 3)

Taylor, S.E. (1981) A categorization approach to stereotyping, in D.L. Hamilton (ed.), *Cognitive Processes in Stereotyping and Intergroup Behavior*, Hillsdale, NJ: Lawrence Erlbaum Associates

Thelen, E. and Smith, L.B. (1996) *A Dynamic Systems Approach to the Development of Cognition and Action*, Cambridge, MA: MIT Press

The Nuremberg Code (1947), in A. Mitscherlic and F. Mielke (1949) *Doctors of Infamy: The Story of the Nazi Medical Crimes,* New York: Schuman, xxiii-xxv [online] available at: http://www.cirp.org/library/ethics/nuremberg [accessed 14 October 2010]

The UN Convention on the Rights of the Child (1989), adopted and opened for signature, ratification and accession by General Assembly resolution 44/25 of 20 November 1989. Entry into force 2 September 1990, in accordance to Article 49) [online] available at: http://www2.ohchr.org/english/law/crc.htm [accessed 14 November 2010]

The WMA Declaration of Helsinki (1964/2008) *Ethical Principles for Medical Research Involving Human Subjects*, [online] available at: http://www.wma.net/en/30publications/10policies/b3/index.html [accessed 14 November 2010]

Thomas, M.R. (2003) *Blending Qualitative and Quantitative Research Methods in Theses and Dissertations*, Thousand Oaks, CA: Corwin Press

Thompson, P. (2008) Children and young people: voices in visual research, in P. Thomson (ed.), *Doing Visual Research with Children and Young People*, London: Routledge

Tudge, J. and Hogan, D. (2005) An ecological approach to observations of children's everyday lives, in S. Greene and D. Hogan (eds), *Researching Children's Experience*, London: Sage

Vasta, R., Haith, M.M. and Miller, S.A. (1999) *Child Psychology: The Modern Science* (3rd edn), New York: J. Wiley & Sons

Vygotsky, L.S. (1978) *Mind in Society: The Development of Higher Psychological Processes* (ed. and trans. M. Cole, V. John-Steiner, S. Scribner and E. Souberman), Cambridge, MA: Harvard University Press

Vygotsky, L.S. (1986) *Thought and Language* (trans. and ed. A. Kozulin), Cambridge, MA: The MIT Press [Russian edition published in Moscow, 1934]

Warming, H. (2005) Participant observation: a way to learn about children's perspectives, in A. Clark, A.T. Kjørholt and P. Moss (eds), *Beyond Listening*, Bristol: Policy Press

Watson, J.B. (1930) *Behaviorism* (rev. edn), Chicago, IL: University of Chicago Press

Webster, R. (2010) Listening to and learning from children's perspectives, in J. Moyles (ed.), *Thinking about Play: Developing a Reflective Approach*, Maidenhead: McGraw Hill/Open University Press

Weick, K.E. (1985) Systematic observational methods, in G. Lindzey and E. Aronson (eds), *The Handbook of Social Psychology* (3rd edn), New York: Random House

Weir, R. (1962) *Language in the Crib*, The Hague: Mouton

Wells, G. (1999) *Dialogic Inquiry: Toward a Sociocultural Practice and Theory of Education*, London: Cambridge University Press

West, P. (1972) *Words for a Deaf Daughter*, Harmondsworth: Penguin Books

Whalley, M. (2001) *Involving Parents in their Children's Learning*, London: Sage

Willig, C. (2001) *Introducing Qualitative Research in Psychology: Adventures in Theory and Method*, Buckingham: Open University Press

Winter, R., Buck, A. and Sobiechowska, P. (1999) *Professional Experience and the Investigative Imagination*, London: Routledge

Wolcott, H. (2001) *Writing Up Qualitative Research* (2nd edn), London: Sage

Woodhead, M. (1996) *In Search of the Rainbow: Pathways to Quality in Large Scale Programmes for Young Disadvantaged Children*, The Hague: Bernard van Leer Foundation

Woodhead, M., Faulkner, D. and Littleton, K. (1998) *Cultural Worlds of Early Childhood*, London: Routledge

Woolfolk, A., Hughes, M. and Walkup, V. (2008) *Psychology in Education*, Harlow: Pearson

Working Group Against Racism in Children's Resources (WGARCR) (1991) *Guidelines for the Selection and Evaluation of Child Development Books*, London: WGARCR

Worthington, M. (2010) 'This is a *different* calculator – with computer games on': reflecting on children's symbolic play in the digital age, in J. Moyles (ed.), *Thinking about Play: Developing a Reflective Approach*, Maidenhead: McGraw Hill/Open University Press

Yin, R.K. (2003) *Case Study Research: Design and Methods* (3rd edn), London, Thousand Oaks CA and New Delhi: Sage

Appendix 1

Sample participant information letter and consent form

Participant information letter

(On institutional headed paper, if required)

(Name and address of parent/carer)   Date

Dear . . .,

I am a student at . . . (name of institution) where I am reading for a degree in early childhood studies. As part of my studies I am required to observe a young child to understand child development and my own learning. The headteacher, . . . (name), and the staff of . . . (name of school/nursery) have kindly agreed that I may conduct my observations in the nursery class. I have visited the school and I would like to observe your son/daughter . . . (name), but I will not do so without your permission.

. . . (child's name) joined . . . (name of nursery/school) three weeks ago and I am interested in observing her/him to understand how young children experience the transition from the familiar home environment to the new nursery environment.

I would like to observe . . . (child's name) for an hour each week for six weeks. The observations will take place in the nursery class in the presence of staff during normal play activities. I will keep notes, which I will share with my fellow students and my tutor as part of my learning activities. All information will be anonymous and confidential. I will use pseudonyms and will not disclose information that may allow identification of . . . (child's name).

The observation notes will be used for my final assessment to demonstrate my own learning and understanding about young children's transitions from home to nursery. I will not use the data to make any judgements about . . . (child's name) development, learning, behaviour or progress, as I am not a qualified professional. Your permission for me to observe . . . (child's name) is, however, important for me – it will assist me in my learning and in my future professional knowledge and skills. Enclosed is a letter from my tutor to confirm that I am required to make an observational study of a child as part of my course, and a copy of my Criminal Records Bureau (CRB) clearance showing that I have passed the necessary checks for working with children. If you would like to discuss this request further, please do not hesitate to contact me at . . . (phone no./or address – students are advised to give their institutional rather than their personal address).

I hope that you will carefully consider my request and, if you agree, sign the enclosed copies of the consent form.

Yours sincerely,

(Student's name)

Consent form

I agree to my child (name) . . . . being observed by . . . (student's name). I have read the written participant information that . . . (student's name) has provided me with and all my questions have been answered to my satisfaction. I understand that all information is confidential and will be used for learning purposes and/or publication anonymously. I am free to ask any questions before and during the observations and I understand that I am free to withdraw my consent at any time, for any reason and without prejudice.

(Insert here details about photographs and video-recording, if relevant – e.g. who owns them; how you will save them and for how long; how you will be using them.)

I have been provided with an explanatory letter and understand I will be given a copy of this form to keep.

(Name of parent/guardian)

Print .... Sign .... Date ....

If you wish to withdraw your consent at any time, please sign the section below the dotted line and return it to me. Thank you.

(Student's name)

I wish to withdraw my consent

(Name of parent/guardian)

Print .... Sign .... Date ....

Appendix 2

Segmented observation record and assigned categories

Segmented observation record	Initial and (in shaded rows) emerging assigned categories
1. Raya is two years and one month old.	1. Other (Not development skills-Age)
2. She sits in front of a box with sensory resources (treasure basket).	2. Motor (Static position)
3. She picks up objects one at a time.	3. Motor skills (Fine)
4. Looks at them, waves them, listens to them and places them next to her.	4. Cognitive (Visual, kinetic and auditory exploration)
5. She chats to herself.	5. Language (Self-talk)
6. Words are mainly unrecognisable.	6. Language (Self-talk/Unrecognisable words)
7. Occasionally I recognise words such as ball, box, key.	7. Language (Self-talk/Recognisable words)
8. All her chatter is very animated, with a range of intonation.	8. Emotional (Expression)
9. She moves on to playing with objects together in the basket.	9. Cognitive (Combining objects)
10. She picks up the pan, puts the metal whisk in the pan and then tries other metal objects together.	10. Cognitive (Sorting)
11. She tries to put the wooden whisk into the pan. It didn't fit.	11. Cognitive (Encountering problems)
12. She went back to emptying and investigating objects one at a time.	12. Cognitive (Looking for solution?)
13. Raya left the treasure basket then quickly returned and continued emptying more objects from it one at a time.	13. Cognitive (problem solving?)
14. She then started reading the mini-book to herself.	14. Cognitive (Making connections?) or (Other – perceptual attention?)

(Continued)

Segmented observation record	Initial and (in shaded rows) emerging assigned categories
15. When she finishes reading the book she says, 'Bye-bye book.'	15. Language (Self-talk/Full sentences)
16. She continues emptying objects one at a time from the basket.	16. Motor skills (Fine)
17. Each time she chats to herself, as if explaining what she had got or was doing.	17. Language (Self-talk)
18. She puts the book in the treasure basket. Then puts the other objects back in the basket.	18. Social (Pro-social/Sense of order)
19. Chats to herself, as if she was naming objects as she did it.	19. Language (Self-talk)
20. Raya leaves the activity and goes to play in the home corner.	20. Social (Independence?)

Appendix 3

A revised analytical framework

Revised emerging coded themes	Revised emerging coded categories
Motor development (MOT)	MOT-GR (Gross motor skills)
	MOT-FI (Fine motor skills)
Language development (LANG)	LANG-SW (Single words)
	LANG-CW (Combination of words)
	LANG-FS (Full sentences)
	LANG-ST (Self-talk)
	LANG-ST/UW (Self-talk/Unrecognisable words)
	LANG-ST/RW (Self-talk/Recognisable words)
	LANG-FS/ST (Self-talk/Full sentences)
Communication (COM)	COM-V (Verbal)
	COM-NV (Non-verbal)
Cognitive development (COGN)	COGN-EXPL (Exploration)
	COGN-EXPL/VKA (Exploration/Visual, Kinetic and Auditory
	COGN-PS (Problem solving)
	COGN-SORT (Sorting)
	COGN-CO (Combining objects)
	COGN-EP (Encountering problems)
	COGN-LS (Looking for solutions)
	COGN-CS (Cognitive shift)
Emotional development (EMOT)	EMOT-EE (Expressing emotions)
	EMOT-RE (Responding to emotions)

(Continued)

Revised emerging coded themes	Revised emerging coded categories
Social development (SOC)	SOC-PR/SO (Pro-social/Sense of order)
	SOC-PR/ID (Pro-social/Independence)
Other emerging themes (OTHER) – Perceptual	OTHER-ATT (Attention)
Other emerging themes (OTHER) – Not developmental information	OTHER-AGE (Age)

Appendix 4

Sample of a front sheet for assessed work

Child's name (pseudonym):

Age:

Gender:

Place of observation:

Date and time:

Duration of observation:

Number of observation, if part of a series of observations:

Other contextual information:

Attached informed consent, enclosed in an envelope

Index

CPSIA information can be obtained
at www.ICGtesting.com
Printed in the USA
FSOW04n0648130717
36271FS

9 781405 824675